A Deeper Wisdom
The 12 Steps from a Woman's Perspective

PATRICIA LYNN REILLY

Girl God Books

©2021 by Patricia Lynn Reilly

ISBN: 978-82-93725-12-1

Cover Art by Arna Baartz

www.thegirlgod.com

Praise for A Deeper Wisdom

"The Higher Power of recovery seemed to be the male God of my childhood past called by another name. My life was unmanageable in many ways when I showed up at my first meeting. Until reading *A Deeper Wisdom* I found it easy to believe that a male higher power would deliver me from the mess I was in. Men have always been my fix. It's strange that my recovery sponsors didn't get it. They were asking me to replace my addiction to men with a surrender to a higher power who would rescue me. Unpacking internalized misogyny became an essential component of my ADW journey." -Susan

"*A Deeper Wisdom* helped me rethink AA's Twelve Steps from my perspective. I rewrote them, using concepts of "god" more helpful to me. Now I sit in meetings without resentment because I've altered what didn't work for me." -Jenny

"*A Deeper Wisdom* taught me how to tap into my own inner resources. With the book's help, I've let go of the belief that I am fundamentally ill-equipped to deal with my life challenges without the assistance of an expert." -Katie

"Through *A Deeper Wisdom*, I realized that I do not have the time or energy to get caught up in the swirls of my past. My current life demands all my energy. Whenever I begin to obsess about my past life, I re-establish conscious contact with my breath and body, and then turn toward one of my current projects." -Loretta

"Inspired by Patricia's book I was ready to finally name a missing and unrecognized piece in women's recovery experience—that 'higher power' may work for men, but that a woman's spirit, soul, and life resonates with a 'deeper wisdom.' Ours is a soul journey of reclaiming our greatness, rooted in and trusting our deeper wisdom." -Anne Wondra, WonderSpirit

A Deeper Wisdom reframes the traditional 12 steps formulated for Alcoholic's Anonymous and used in most offshoots of that original program.

The 12 steps from a woman's perspective are based on a belief in the healing capacity of self-love and self-trust.

Each step affirms our natural impulse toward wholeness, transforming self-criticism into compassion and the suffering that fuels habit-energy into joy.

The use of "deeper" in the book's title acknowledges that a woman's journey is one of descent. Instead of looking to a god or higher power outside of our lives, we look deep within to reclaim forgotten aspects of ourselves.

The use of "wisdom" acknowledges that in our descent we rediscover the original wisdom that orchestrated our days and development in the very beginning of life. Deeper Wisdom restores us to wholeness and to a loving relationship with ourselves and others.

CONTENTS

Introduction: A Personal Story

My awakening came late in time. I missed the second wave of feminism in the 1960s and 1970s. I was immersed in fundamentalist traditions that kept me isolated from the political movements in the wider culture. I was dealing with the aftermath of growing up in a severely dysfunctional home, children's shelter, and orphanage—the kind of situations no one wanted to hear about because they are "so depressing."

I was managing depression and my disheveled inner landscape with food and relationships. These habits of behavior kept me comatose until I was ready to walk through my personal past. I also finished high school and college successfully, launched a private day school, found great joy in teaching, and courageously entered a marriage. Light and darkness always dance together in our lives.

I was not alone. In circles of women, I heard stories of other women whose "consciousness raising" was precipitated by real life challenges. The "knight in shining armor" mythology shattered as they divorced and became the sole financial and emotional provider for their children. They sought support at a local women's center and began to listen to women's stories, shedding the competitive attitudes of a lifetime.

Their therapists suggested they read *The Second Sex* or *The Creation of Patriarchy* and they were stunned that women had written such powerful treatises that they had known nothing about. They stumbled into self-help meetings, as I did, where someone said "goddess" instead of the compulsory "god" in the Twelve Step readings, and we wondered how the reader got the courage to commit such a heretical act.

The Twelve Step Community

Twelve Step meetings punctuated my life from college graduation onward. I held off marriage as long as possible until I was drawn into the rescue drama of the minister's wayward son. He had "returned to god" and was recovering from alcoholism in Alcoholics Anonymous. He was a perfect candidate for my unexamined caretaker patterns. I attended Al-Anon to support him.

At Twelve Step meetings I found the Christian version of god. The "Our Father," a Christian prayer, was said at the close of most meetings. And the program's emphasis on shortcomings, character defects, and ego-deflation felt familiar to me as it was an extension of the sin-based teachings I'd been inhaling since childhood. I was fundamentally "diseased" and the remedy was to turn my will and life over to the god. I had no trouble turning my life and will over to *him*.

In transition after the divorce, while attending Princeton Seminary, my healing journey in Adult Children of Alcoholics began. The Al-Anon of my married years had not touched the wounds of my childhood as the program's primary focus was how to cope with an alcoholic spouse or child. During the 1980s, influenced by psychologists steeped in family systems theory, alcoholism began to be understood as a family disease affecting all family members. Al-Anon responded to the new research by establishing ACA – Adult Children of Alcoholics.

In ACA meetings, I took responsibility for my healing journey by exploring the nature and impact of alcoholism on our family system. Over time, I realized that I didn't cause the craziness in my family of origin—alcoholism had a life of its own within our family. Acknowledging childhood's influence on my adult life, I chose to walk through my past to heal into the present. And this meant confronting my compulsive eating.

One of the ways I coped with the alcoholic family, children's shelter, orphanage—and later, the gap between my insecurity and the opportunities offered to me as a gifted young person—was to eat compulsively. One way or another, I found huge amounts of sugary food and ate like a junkie shoots up her heroin. I literally hid in closets to eat and dropped out of life for days and months at a time as the binges coincided with the cyclical depression I'd lived with since childhood.

In the pauses between relationships and accomplishments, I was reminded of my swirling inner life of unexpressed feelings, unacknowledged memories, and untapped potential. To get caught up in the swirl of a project or life of another made perfect sense. The prospect of living my own life from the inside out frightened me. I ate to avoid the awesome responsibility of coming home to myself.

When I finally landed in Overeaters Anonymous, I was exhausted from swirling in the food. I reached out for OA's healing resources and was given the tools of self-care and self-soothing that I had not received in my childhood. Its suggested food plan freed me to walk through my past and heal into the present.

Although I received many gifts of support and insight from the Twelve Step community during my years of attendance, its emphasis on ego-deflation, a concept designed by men based on their experience of themselves, was always a concern to me. Perhaps ego-deflation is an appropriate remedy for men who consider pride to be their besetting sin, but I came to believe that self-acceptance and self-trust were more appropriate remedies for women whose besetting "sins" were self-loathing and self-criticism.

I desired a non-shaming, non-hierarchical framework within which to wrestle with my habits of behavior. I rewrote the 12 Steps from an inner perspective, recognizing that my journey was an inward one. Instead of looking to another god or higher power outside of my life for salvation, I longed to return home to myself—to grow in knowledge and love of myself—to accept and trust myself. I wasn't interested in ascending to enlightened states of being that involved the denial of the self. I was compelled to descend—to look deep within to reclaim forgotten aspects of myself.

Releasing the shame of a lifetime, I reached beneath the obsession with flaws, beneath the accomplishments that masked my sense of unworthiness, beneath the years of alienation from myself, toward the goodness at my center. I discovered that the good was embedded within me. As I embraced my original goodness, my inner spaces were cleared out and reclaimed as my own. I found rest within my own life and accepted all of myself as worthy.

From a self-possessed center, I refused to embrace any set of principles based on the belief in my fundamental sinfulness and defectiveness or on the necessity of ego deflation, humiliation, or the surrender of my natural impulses. Instead, I re-framed the 12 Steps based on my belief in original goodness and the necessity of self-love and self-trust. Each step now answers the question, "what's good and right about me" and affirms my natural impulse toward healing and wholeness.

As I was writing *A Deeper Wisdom*, I invited a community of recovering women to join me in the process. Studying pre-patriarchal history together, we discovered a courageous community of women whose experience and stories, ideas and images, creativity and outrage become healing resources for us. No longer asking the question "what's wrong with me," we stepped outside of male-dominated history and thought and immersed ourselves in women's history, philosophy, theology,

4

creativity, and recovery. We received Gerda Lerner's strong challenge:

> "To step outside of patriarchal thought means being skeptical toward every known system of thought and toward our own thought, which was trained in the patriarchal tradition. It means developing intellectual courage, the courage to stand alone.
>
> Perhaps the greatest challenge to thinking women is the challenge to move from the desire for safety and approval to the most "unfeminine" quality of all—intellectual arrogance, the supreme hubris which asserts to itself the right to reorder the world. The hubris of the god-makers, the hubris of the male system-builders."

We've been warned against exhibiting 'hubris' all of our lives. Gerda Lerner supports us to be full of ourselves for the salvation of our beloved planet, which is out of balance and in danger of annihilating itself. Inspired by her powerful words, I asserted my right to reorder the world by rewriting the 12 Steps. *A Deeper Wisdom* was written for all women wrestling with habits of behaviors that inhibit the full expression of their heart, mind, and spirit.

A Life-Practice for all Women

Whether or not you have ever set foot in a recovery meeting is irrelevant—*A Deeper Wisdom* is for all women. We have all lost our way at times. We have all wrestled with habits of thought and behavior that troubled and challenged us. We have all written self-improvement lists and committed to diet regimens recognizing that some of our habits did not support the life we wanted.

A Deeper Wisdom is a powerful woman-affirming life-practice for all of us. It is based on the belief in our original goodness and in the healing capacity of self-love and self-trust. Each step affirms our natural impulse toward wholeness, transforming self-criticism into self-compassion and the suffering that fuels habit-energy into joy.

The 12 Steps introduced in this book were written from an inner perspective, recognizing that life is lived from the inside out and that the most essential aspect of our human journey is an inward one. Instead of looking to another god or higher power outside of our lives for salvation, we return home to ourselves and accept the responsibility for waking up and becoming aware of our thoughts, feelings, behaviors, lives, and relationships.

A Deeper Wisdom's version of the 12 Steps invites us to descend —to look deep within to reclaim forgotten aspects of ourselves. As we descend, we notice an unmistakable design flowing from the depths of us. We notice that this flow of deep wisdom was faithful even in the midst of difficulties and apparent detours from what was healthy and good.

The journey home to ourselves begins with a deep breath and the courageous vulnerability of acknowledging that we have lost our way and need guidance to find our way home. On the journey home, we are restored to peace, sanity, and a loving relationship with ourselves.

Softly and tenderly. Wisdom is calling. Calling for you and for me.
Come home. Come home. All who are weary come home.
Softly and tenderly. Wisdom is calling.
Calling, O woman, come home.

Chapter 1

In the Very Beginning:
ADW's Woman-Affirming Perspectives and Steps

Four perspectives guided my re-conceptualization of the traditional 12 Steps. Each woman-affirming perspective will be examined carefully in this chapter and glimpsed in every transformational resource introduced throughout this book. I have personalized them here as an invitation to ready your mind, heart, and spirit to begin the poignant journey toward deepening self-awareness and essential reclamation of the amazing resources within you.

1. *Your healing task is not to become a new, improved, or changed person. Rather, it is to reclaim your essential self* kernal *in all its fullness.*

2. *Discover the way home to yourself in a quiet descent into the richness of your inner life. In the descent, you will reunite with your essential self and reclaim your natural resources: body, breath, and inner life.*

3. *Be empowered as you remember the truth about yourself and become skillful at accessing the resources and resilience embedded within that truth in every season and situation of your life.*

4. *Having discovered the way home, embrace the essential connection between self-love and the love of others, and* love of My life *experience your life and relationships from the inside out.*

ADW PERSPECTIVE 1: THE JOURNEY

A woman's healing task is not to become a new, improved, or changed person. Rather, it is to reclaim her natural and essential self in all its fullness.

7

I had two very special seven-year-old friends, Moizee and Carson. They are exquisite young adults now—in their childhood they were my teachers. They reminded me of a time in the very beginning of my life when I was full of myself. As we spent time talking, singing, playing, and exploring together, snapshots of that earlier time passed through my mind's eye, fragments of a forgotten time.

Yes, in the very beginning of her life the girl-child is full of herself. Her days are meaningful and unfold according to a deep wisdom that resides within her. It faithfully orchestrates her movements from crawling to walking to running, her sounds from garbles to single words to sentences, and her knowing of the world through her sensual connection to it.

Her purpose is clear: to live fully in the abundance of her life. With courage, she explores her world. Her ordinary life is interesting enough. Every experience is filled with wonder and awe. It is enough to listen to the rain dance and count the peas on her plate. Ordinary life is her teacher, challenge, and delight.

She says a big YES to Life as it pulsates through her body. With excitement, she explores her body. She is unafraid of channeling strong feelings through her. She feels her joy, sadness, anger, and fear. She is pregnant with her own life. She is content to be alone. She touches the depths of her uniqueness. She loves her mind. She expresses her feelings. She likes herself when she looks in the mirror.

She trusts her vision of the world and expresses it. With wonder and delight, she paints a picture, creates a dance, and makes up a song. To give expression to what she sees is as natural as her breathing. And when challenged, she is not lost for words. She has a vocabulary to speak about her experience. She speaks from her heart. She voices her truth. She has no fear, no sense that to do it her way is wrong or dangerous.

She is a warrior. It takes no effort for her to summon up her courage, to arouse her spirit. With her courage, she solves problems. She is capable of carrying out any task that confronts her. She has everything she needs within the grasp of her mind and imagination. With her spirit, she changes what doesn't work for her. She says "I don't like that person" when she doesn't, and "I like that person" when she does. She says no when she doesn't want to be hugged. She takes care of herself.

What's Wrong with Me?

As I celebrated the remarkable capacities of Moizee and Carson, I became aware of critical words from my childhood and adolescence, echoing across the decades to challenge their fullness, and my own. These deeply imprinted words recount what happened to the precious being I once was, we once were, in the very beginning of our lives. Over time, the inner voice that led us into wonder-filled explorations was replaced by critical voices.

As a result, the girl-child's original vision is narrowed; she sees the world as everyone else sees it. She loses her ability to act spontaneously; she acts as expected. Her original trust in herself is shattered; she waits to be told how to live. Her original spunk is exiled; she learns that it is dangerous to venture outside the lines. Her original goodness is twisted and labeled unnatural-unfeminine-too intense-evil by the adults in her life.

She will grow up asking, "What's wrong with me?" This question regularly punctuates women's lives as they search far and wide for someone to give them an answer, for someone to offer them a magical insight, treatment, or cure. We have learned a criticism-based way of perceiving ourselves and relating to the world. As a result, our automatic tendency is to feel inadequate, that we are never quite good enough no matter what we do.

The human life journey has been described in a variety of ways by secular, religious, and philosophical systems of thought. The viewpoint underlying the ADW Step Process recognizes that a woman's journey takes her through three seasons of life, which are outlined here and expanded upon by wise and insightful writers and teachers in this chapter and in each subsequent chapter of *A Deeper Wisdom*.

1. The Very Beginning: Our Natural Endowment | At Home

This is the season, often short-lived, when we love ourselves and have access to the resources and capacities necessary to support resilient living.

> "Dear Sisters, please remember: The jewel is in your bosom. Why look for it somewhere else?" -Japanese Folk Saying

> "At the buried core of women's identity is a distinct and vital self-first articulated in childhood." -Emily Hancock, *The Girl Within*

> "I have a strong connection to my daughter. She reminds me of the girl child I once was. She is perfect. I look at her and I don't see any flaws. What I celebrate in her reminds me of my true nature. As I parent her as I wish I'd been parented, the child in me is healed." -Erin Louise Stewart

2. Forgetting: Conformity-Based Dictates | Away from Home

This is the season when life's influences and expectations veil our self-love and replace it with self-criticism. We become "formula females."

> "Our psychological being has been severed from our biological selves for so long that we are completely cut off from our true natures." -Elinor Gadon

> "For over a century, the edge of adolescence has been identified as a time of heightened psychological risk for girls. Girls at this time have been observed to lose their vitality,

their resilience, their immunity to depression, their sense of themselves and their character." -Carol Gilligan, *Meetings at the Crossroads*

"By the time they are seventeen many young women have surrendered their ambitions to a growing need for affection and their autonomy to an emotional dependence on the approval and good will of others. At seventeen the young woman is well on her way to being a formula female."
-Madonna Kolbenschlag, *Kiss Sleeping Beauty Goodbye*

3. Remembering: Reclaiming What We Once Knew | The Return Home

This is the season when we reunite with our essential self and natural endowments, and relearn how to be, live, and love from the inside out.

"There was a time when you walked alone, full of laughter. You bathed bare-bellied. You say you have lost all recollection of it, remember! You say there are not words to describe it; you say it does not exist. But remember! Make an effort to remember! Or failing that, invent." -Monique Wittig, *Les Guerilliers*

"When we live from within outward, in touch with our inner power, we become responsible to ourselves in the deepest sense. As we recognize our deepest feelings, we give up being satisfied with suffering, self-negation, and numbness, which seem like our society's only alternatives." -Audre Lorde

Each book and resource I've written reminds women of these three seasons and invites them to return home to the "very beginning" when they loved themselves. This "returning" involves ousting two questions "what's wrong with me" and "who will save me" from our hearts, minds, and bodies. The ADW Process affirms that we are originally blessed, not cursed; that strength, creativity, and resilience reside within each of us; and that these

11

inherent qualities are powerful enough to heal our injuries and transform our ineffective behaviors.

ADW PERSPECTIVE 2: THE DESCENT

A woman discovers the way home to herself in a quiet descent into the richness of her own life. In the descent, she reunites with her essential self and natural resources.

In the very beginning of life, you were acquainted with the exquisite natural resources of your breath, body, and inner life. You breathed deeply into your belly. You loved your body. You were in touch with the wisdom within your own life.

Over time, however, the girl-child becomes disconnected from the "home" within her. Caught in the swirls of others, twisted in the shapes of others, depleted by the demands of others, she becomes outer-directed and loses touch with herself. Her breath becomes shallow. She ignores her body. She looks to saviors outside of herself for salvation and validation, forgetting the rich resources within her.

In the fullness of time, we become dizzy from swirling; our lives ache from being twisted out of shape; and our spirits become depleted from servicing others with our energy and attention. Weary, we reach out to a counselor, spiritual community, or self-help group. We are offered information, insight, and tools of support. We are inspired by the experience, strength, and hope of others who are turning toward their own lives with vulnerability, courage, and truth.

Insight, information, and camaraderie point us in the right direction, but the journey begins as we turn toward our own lives and look within to re-connect to our natural resources: breath, woman-body, and inner life. Based on this conviction, we include the "Home Is Always Waiting" Meditation in each ADW group and individual session and I wrote an entire book focused on this principle and the meditation it inspired.

Home is always waiting. It is as near as a conscious breath, conscious contact with your woman-body, and a descent into the abundant resources of your inner life. The meaning, recovery, and transformation you seek 'out there' is found within your own heart, mind, body, and life. It is accessed in the present moment and released into your experience with each mindful breath. Return home often—you have everything you need there.

Home is Always Waiting: Return Home to Your Breath

"About 21,600 times a day, you have the opportunity to catch the wave of your breath: mindfully inhaling and mindfully exhaling with a gentle smile and full awareness." -Michelle Levey, *Simple Meditation and Relaxation*

"Most of us live on a beggar's ration of air. The average person inhales one pint of air per breath, while our lungs can actually contain seven pints when fully expanded. This is one of the reasons that the range and depth of our experiences disappoint our longings." -Margo Anand, *The Art of Sexual Ecstasy*

"Daring to breathe is actually daring to live. As we all know, when we cease breathing, we die. As long as we are alive, the depth of our breathing determines the amount of life force we bring into ourselves. Given only a stingy amount of oxygen, our bodies, hearts, and minds will not function well." -Sue Patton Thoele

Home is Always Waiting: Return Home to Your Body

"Body wisdom contains the essential truths about what matters most to a woman. Body wisdom especially amplifies the inherent sacred relationship between a woman and the deep feminine." -Paula M. Reeves, *Women's Intuition*
"Your body can be considered a reservoir of cellular memory, wisdom, and guidance. If you attend it, it can richly reward

your journey with understanding about your deepest being and about the ways you might find healing and wholeness."
-Marion Woodman, *Coming Home to Myself*

Home is Always Waiting: Return Home to Your Inner Life

"Transformation comes from looking deep within, to a state that exists before fear and isolation arise, the state in which we are inviolably whole just as we are. We connect to ourselves, to our own true experience, and discover there that to be alive means to be whole." -Sharon Salzberg, *Voices of Insight*

"Mindfulness practice places us in the stream of wisdom flowing through our inner lives, and there, we make conscious contact with our truest self and clearest thought." -Patricia Lynn Reilly, *Home is Always Waiting*

ADW PERSPECTIVE 3: THE KNOWING

A woman is empowered when she remembers the truth about herself and becomes skillful at accessing the resources and resilience embedded within that truth in every season and situation of her life.

Based on ADW's definition of empowerment, each Step Process will remind you of a particular truth about yourself and provide mindfulness practices to bring inner clarity in support of addressing your historic and current life challenges.

Step 1 will remind you of your original power and how to access it to act on your own behalf and gather the resources necessary to heal into the present.

Step 2 will remind you of your inner wisdom and how to access it to define your own spirituality and reclaim inner sanity and well-being.

Step 3 will remind you of the support available from within your own inner resources and from the communities of support that surround you.

Step 4 will remind you that your interior power is activated by self-awareness. That by acknowledging the past's influence on the present, walking through the past, and healing into the present, you will grow in self-knowledge.

Step 5 will remind you that interior power is strengthened by taking responsibility for your habits of behavior and vowing faithfulness to your own life.

Step 6 will remind you that your life-process is orchestrated by a finely-tuned inner timing—called deeper wisdom. In the fullness of time, when entirely ready, you are freed at a deeper level of your being.

Step 7 will remind you of the importance of staying awake within your own life, meeting each challenge with creativity and taking action on your own behalf with clarity and strength.

Step 8 will remind you of the essential connection between self-love, self-acceptance, and self-responsibility, and the creation and maintenance of healthy relationships.

Step 9 will remind you of your own inner courage to repair, reclaim, or bring closure to the relationships that were harmed by your ineffective behaviors.

Step 10 will remind you to remain absolutely present in your daily life by turning toward your life with mindfulness, accountability, and gratitude.

Step 11 will remind you of the necessity of maintaining conscious contact with yourself as you live in harmony from the inside out.

Step 12 will remind you of the purposefulness of a conscious life as it is lived from the inside out in wisdom, truth, and clear thought.

ADW PERSPECTIVE 4: THE CONNECTION

Having discovered the way home, we embrace the essential connection between love of self and others, and experience our lives and relationships from the inside out.

Throughout the ADW Process, you'll be invited to reach out to the communities of support. In isolation our negative habits of behavior thrive. In healthy community our negative habits of behavior are no longer needed. As we grow in self-love, acceptance, and compassion, we are able to engage fully with others on the journey.

Self-love: Your capacity to love others is in direct proportion to how deeply you love yourself. The ADW Process invites you to gaze upon your past and present, ideas and emotions, resources and capacities, injury and exquisite potential, and your body and its needs with loving kindness. In this way, your capacity to love will deepen.

Self-acceptance: Your capacity to live non-judgmentally is in direct proportion to how deeply you accept yourself. The ADW Process invites you to descend into your richly textured humanity in all its gift and challenge, turning a merciful eye toward all that you discover. In this way, your capacity to live compassionately will deepen.

Self-interest: Your capacity to be available to others is in direct proportion to how substantially you are available to yourself. The ADW Process invites you to turn toward yourself with interest and attention to acknowledge your own feelings, thoughts, and perceptions and to offer yourself support through life's challenges and celebrations. In this way, your capacity to be available to others will deepen.

Self-possession: Your capacity to participate in your relationships is in direct proportion to how fully you participate in your life. The ADW Process invites you to participate in your own life, meeting each challenge with creativity, and taking action on your own behalf with clarity and strength. In this way, your capacity to participate meaningfully in your significant relationships will deepen.

Self-loyalty: Your capacity to remain faithful to others is in direct proportion to the depth of your self-loyalty. The ADW Process invites you to maintain loyalty to yourself, preserving allegiance even in the face of opposition. In this way, your capacity to sustain interest in others and remain faithful to them will deepen.

THE STEPS REWRITTEN

The ADW Steps are listed below. Each Step will also be explored in-depth in its own chapter.

The Twelve Steps from a Woman's Perspective

Step 1: Caught in the swirl of my habits of behavior, I have lost touch with myself and my life has become unmanageable. I reach out for support. This is a brave action on my own behalf.

Step 2: I have come to believe in the deep wisdom of my own inner life. I stop flailing and am restored to the sanity of a loving and respectful relationship with myself.

Step 3: I turn my current situation over to the deep wisdom that flows in and through my life. One self-caring step at a time, I unravel my harmful habits of behavior, and the thoughts that hold them in place.

Step 4: Turning a merciful eye toward myself, I inventory both my life-affirming and ineffective habits of behaviors, and identify the habits of thought that inspire them.

Step 5: In the company of trustworthy allies, I celebrate my life-affirming behaviors, accept responsibility for my ineffective behaviors, and make a commitment to my transformation.

Step 6: I am entirely ready to deepen my inner well-being by relinquishing my negative habits of behavior and cultivating new thoughts to inspire healthier behaviors and outcomes.

Step 7: My life journey is orchestrated by my own inner wisdom. In the fullness of time, I am transformed at a deeper level of my being. I actively participate in this process.

Step 8: Certain that I love myself, I welcome clarity in my relationships. I acknowledge those who were hurt by my ineffective habits of behavior.

Step 9: Having forgiven myself, I take active responsibility by making amends to those I harmed except when to do so would further injure them or others.

Step 10: Choosing to be present in my own life, I acknowledge the gifts and challenges of the day, celebrate my life-affirming behaviors, and take responsibility for my ineffective ones.

Step 11: Through mindful reflection, I place myself in the stream of wisdom flowing through my life. I make conscious contact with my truest self and clearest thought.

Step 12: Having had an awakening as a result of these Steps, I practice these steps in all my affairs by living in harmony with my deep wisdom, true self, and clear thought.

An Evolving Relationship to The Steps

Those of us who find our way into the 12 Step community are usually in crisis when we first arrive. While in crisis, we are overwhelmed by our troubling condition. After we achieve a level of clear thinking by abstaining from our bottom line addictive behavior, we become aware of the formative experiences and habits of thought beneath our troubling and ineffective behaviors.

We begin our quest for deeper meaning and holistic health. Eventually we use the Steps "in all our affairs," embracing them as a tool of support in everyday life. Through each of these three stages, our understanding of the Steps evolves. Note Sarah's use of the Steps at different stages of her recovery from compulsive overeating.

I. In Crisis

Sarah was overwhelmed by her negative, troubling condition.

Step 1: I am powerless over my mental obsession and eating compulsion. My self-destructive use of food cannot be willed away. I attended an OA meeting.

Step 2: I have come to believe that the group will restore me to sane eating.

Step 3: I let go of the obsessive focus on my eating. I will attend three meetings a week. I turn my obsession over to the group and its tools of support.

II. The Search for Meaning

Sarah became aware of the formative experiences and habits of thought beneath her ineffective behaviors.

Step 1: I can't change the fact that I was born into an alcoholic home and that the formative experiences of my mother's helplessness and my father's violence shaped my thoughts, emotions, and behaviors. One of the ways I coped during a turbulent childhood was to eat compulsively.

Step 2: I have come to believe that healing resources are available to me. I will be restored to a loving relationship with my body.

Step 3: I turn myself over to care of these healing resources. I spend time in a community of support and listen to my body's needs and meet them.

III. Practicing the Steps in All Our Affairs

Sarah eventually used the Steps to support her wellness in everyday life.

Step 1: I cannot change my body's fluctuating cycles and monthly cravings.

Step 2: I believe that dietary supports are available to reduce cravings.

Step 3: I turn my cravings over to these dietary supports.

If you are in the crisis stage, work through the ADW Step Process with a particular habit of behavior/addiction in mind. Use this process:

1. Identify your bottom line addictive behavior. For example:

    "I compulsively eat sugar."

    "I compulsively use my credit cards to purchase things I don't need."

2. Define your abstinence:

    "I will abstain from eating sugar one day at a time. I will call a sponsor / friend daily to reaffirm this commitment."

    "I will abstain from incurring unsecured debt one day at a time. I will call a sponsor / friend daily to reaffirm this commitment."

If you are in Stage II ("Meaning") or Stage III ("In All Our Affairs"), allow your understanding of the Steps to expand beyond your habit of behavior. Focus on the ordinary situations and challenges of life as you work through the ADW Step Process.

If you've never encountered the 12 Steps, use ADW's reworking of them as a powerful life-practice, affirming your original goodness and activating the healing capacity of your own self-love and self-trust. Each step affirms your original wholeness, transforming self-criticism into self-compassion and suffering into joy.

Imagine a woman who discovers the way home to herself.
A woman who descends into her own inner life.
Who reunites with her essential self and reclaims her natural capacities.

Imagine a woman who acknowledges the past's influence on the present.
A woman who has walked through her past.
Who has healed into the present.

Imagine yourself as this woman as you continue to read A Deeper Wisdom.

Chapter 2

Interior Power: Self-Awareness and Self-Management

A Deeper Wisdom is a journey you take to develop the positive self-belief and interior power necessary to be restored to a loving and respectful relationship with yourself.

A Deeper Wisdom is a set of skills you learn to assist you in managing your thoughts, feelings, behaviors, attitudes, and relationships in order to act successfully on your own behalf.

The ADW Process cannot give you power. You already have plenty of power. You have interior power. Every human being does. We tend to forget about our interior power over time. We begin to live our lives based on external expectations, opinions, and limitations, and lose touch with our own power. *A Deeper Wisdom* will remind you of your own interior power and how to activate, manage, and strengthen it.

SELF-AWARENESS: ACTIVATING YOUR INTERIOR POWER

Interior power is activated by self-awareness. A truly powerful woman knows herself. She's aware of her strengths and weaknesses, thoughts and feelings, and habits and patterns. A truly powerful woman is curious, and through her daily mindfulness practice is always learning something new about herself.

We have opportunities each day to increase self-awareness. If we pay attention to the ingredients of the self—our reactions and responses, thoughts and feelings, habits and patterns—as we interact with family, friends, and co-workers, we'll learn a lot about ourselves. As you prepare to explore the ADW 12 Steps, note what you have already learned about the ingredients of your *self*. Allow the sample responses from ADW group participants to inspire your own:

Thoughts: I put myself down.   Habits: I eat when stressed.
Feelings: I get angry a lot.   Strengths: I read a lot.
Patterns: I react before thinking. Weaknesses: I give up easily.

Along with the everyday opportunities to learn about the self, there are many practices, techniques, and strategies we can use to increase self-awareness, activate our interior power, and cope with anxiety and stress. As you read through the following list compiled by ADW group participants, note what techniques you have used to learn more about yourself.

- Mindful reflection about a problem, decision, choice, or challenge.
- Walking in the natural world to sort out my thoughts.
- Writing in a journal to download the thoughts and feelings of the day.
- Sharing life's joys and sorrows with a friend or spouse.
- Silent meditation to get guidance and insight from a spiritual source.
- Trying something new and noticing my responses and reactions.

As you read *A Deeper Wisdom,* become more self-aware by paying attention to your thoughts and feelings, responses and reactions, habits and patterns. Notice what thoughts move through your mind as you encounter new ideas about yourself. Notice your automatic reactions when you hear something new or challenging. Notice the feelings triggered in response to the vulnerability of women's stories.

Journal-writing is an excellent self-awareness tool. Prepare a "Self-Awareness Journal" (SAJ) to accompany you through the

ADW Steps. At the conclusion of each reading, record what you noticed and learned about yourself. And consider writing in your SAJ for 5 minutes in the evening, recording what you notice and learn about yourself each day. Allow each day to inspire new questions about yourself.

- Where do my sadness, depression, and anger come from?
- Why do I experience long periods of emotional emptiness?
- Why do I eat (drink, drug) when I'm discouraged?
- What made me happy today?
- Did I blame or take responsibility more often today?

QUALITIES OF SELF-AWARENESS

Jon Kabat-Zinn, MD founded the Stress Reduction Clinic at the University of Massachusetts Medical School. He designed the "Mindfulness-Based Stress Reduction" (MSBR) Program, which includes self, body, breath, and life-awareness techniques. MBSR is taught in medical centers, hospitals, schools, and prisons, and through health maintenance organizations.

Dr. Kabat-Zinn believes that curiosity, self-compassion, and non-judgmental self-acceptance are important ingredients of the kind of self-awareness that activates interior power and reduces stress. I invite you to take these qualities with you as you begin your journey through the ADW Steps.

- Be curious about yourself, about why you think, feel, and act the way you do, about the origins of your habits and patterns.
- Be as compassionate toward yourself and all that you discover as you would be toward someone you love.
- Be honest and accepting of yourself even as you look at some things about yourself that may cause you to feel sad, guilty, angry, or ashamed.

Omar Rahman spent over 29 years in an Alabama maximum-security prison. While there, he and a group of inmates chose to experience a 10-day mindfulness retreat.

They spent the 10 days in silence, turning inward to become aware of all the layers of the self. Omar described his motivation to become self-aware: "I was curious to know where my anger came from, why I got so irritated, why I experienced emotional emptiness, why I got so hung up on this or that craving. I wanted to understand my interior landscape and how to navigate it."

Reading *A Deeper Wisdom* will reach beneath your troublesome behaviors to unearth the thoughts, emotions, mindsets, attitudes, and habits beneath the behaviors. It is this internal landscape that either supports or sabotages our ability to achieve the quality of life we desire. Courage, curiosity, and compassion allowed Omar and the other participants to descend into the silence and explore their internal landscapes.

The movie "The Dhamma Brothers" chronicles their experience. Find the movie online and allow it to inspire your descent into the book's essential explorations.

SELF-MANAGEMENT: STRENGTHENING YOUR INTERIOR POWER

Interior power is strengthened by self-management. A truly powerful woman moves beyond self-awareness to self-management. Through a daily mindfulness practice, she develops the interior skills necessary to manage her thoughts and emotions and to shift her patterns and habits to achieve her goals. A daily mindfulness practice reminds us that the most effective self-management tool is the breath.

Self-management strengthens interior power by increasing our self-esteem, self-respect, and self-confidence. Through self-management our thoughts and actions begin to function as one

valuing of my own spark of Life
Respect for my own spark of life
confidence in the wholeness of life
goodness of life

unit in service of the quality of life, work, and relationships we desire. We grow in self-respect as we live in harmony with our deepest desires, dreams, and goals. We grow in self-confidence every time we successfully manage our thoughts, feelings, patterns, and habits. We grow in positive self-regard as we master new skills and use them to achieve the life we want.

On the other hand, if we don't manage our feelings, thoughts, actions, and patterns, they operate on automatic and can sabotage our dreams, place stress on our personal and professional relationships, and distract us from our goals. Just as we need lots of practice to learn to ride a bike and to speak a second language, we need practice to become skillful at managing our thoughts, feelings, behaviors, and patterns.

A Deeper Wisdom will introduce you to mindfulness-based self-management skills to transform your problematic thoughts, feelings, habits of behavior, relationship patterns, and self-beliefs. The use of these self-management tools will strengthen your interior power and support you to reach the goals and accomplish the outcomes you want. Over time, you will become more skillful at managing your thoughts. Your interior power will be strengthened by your self-management.

A Deeper Wisdom will also remind you of the management tools you have already used to overcome addiction or to change negative patterns of thought or behavior to positive ones. These successful experiences strengthen us to continue our journey of transformation. In your SAJ, list the self-management tools you have used.

- I ask for time to think about something before responding.
- I use recovery tools like HALT if I'm hungry, angry, lonely, or tired.
- I use affirmations to shift negative thought patterns to healthy ones.

- I attend regular meetings to learn ways to manage my addiction.

THOUGHT AWARENESS AND MANAGEMENT

We have more than 30,000 thoughts a day. That's a lot of noisiness in the mind. And as many as 98% of those thoughts are exactly the same thoughts we had yesterday.

These habits of thought have a powerful effect on our lives, choices, health, and success. Some habits of thought support us to achieve our goals. Some habits of thought sabotage our success. Dr. Caroline Leaf puts it this way:

> "When we think angry, frustrated, fearful, self-critical thoughts, they are wired into the brain and therefore change the brain's wiring all day long. Toxic thoughts cause toxic bodies, lives, and futures.
>
> Healthy thoughts cause healthy bodies, lives, and futures. 75%-95% of the mental, emotional, and physical problems experienced today are caused by our thought life."

The thought-track I inherited from my traumatic childhood made it absolutely necessary that I become aware of my habits of thought, and skillful at thought management. I was convinced that what I thought about myself would determine my success at shifting the historic pull toward addiction and dysfunction. I had daily evidence that my habits of thought were shaping how I responded to events, situations, and people, often without my consent.

In the Catholic orphanage, I used the words of the catechism and saints to bring peace to my mind. I memorized the catechism and said the rosary regularly to introduce new thoughts to overcome the abusive chatter. During my high school and college years, I allowed devotional reading and memorization of Bible verses to crowd out the noisiness. Not understanding the origin of these thoughts, I was not very successful at managing them in those early years. I had moments of success, but overall the storm raged unabated.

After college I was fortunate to find my way into 12 Step community. Its emphasis on "stinking thinking" confirmed what I'd noticed about my thoughts. Through regular attendance at Adult Children of Alcoholics meetings, I understood more and more about the origin of my troubling thoughts. I'd been hardwired by the words, attitudes, anger, and abusive behavior of alcoholic and drug-addicted parents and caretakers. Inspired by Alanon's *One Day at a Time* daily reader, I composed my own daily reader with thoughts and affirmations that specifically countered the thoughts in my head.

I also wrote and recorded the "Home is Always Waiting" Meditation. It is filled with healing silence, supportive thoughts, and soothing words. The meditation reaches beneath the inherited noise to the stillness at the center of my being. It invites me to descend into the silence, into my inner landscape with curiosity and acceptance.

Each time I descend into mindful meditation, I receive a gift as new thoughts are born of my natural health and resilience. The new thoughts lead to new words, words of kindness and affirmation. I believe that affirmations are thought seeds that sprout and grow within us and lead to stronger self-acceptance and self-esteem. To master the skill of positive thought cultivation is an important self-management tool.

The word "affirmation" comes from the Latin root word "affirmare," which means "to make firm; to make steady; to strengthen." To affirm is to make firm our resolve to cultivate positive thoughts. Affirmations help detoxify our thoughts and restructure our patterns of thinking. Affirmations assist us to shift immediately from negative thoughts to supportive thoughts. Affirmations are an essential component of the ADW Step Process.

Use your Self-Awareness Journal to keep track of your "30,000" thoughts. Slowly these thoughts will emerge from the shadows of their automatic-ness and make themselves known. Note them in your journal and compose new thoughts to affirm the truth of your being. Here are affirmations based on ADW's re-conceptualization of the Steps. Incorporate them into your daily mindfulness practice, using the breath to deepen the transformative reach of these powerful words.

Step 1 Affirmation: I'm vulnerable—some things I cannot change. With vulnerability, I reach out for assistance. This is a brave action on my own behalf. I'm powerful—some things I can change. With courage, I change the things I can.

Step 2 Affirmation: I'm learning how to access the deep wisdom of my own inner life. I'm restored to the sanity of a loving and respectful relationship with myself.

Step 3 Affirmation: I'm learning how to access the resilience of my own inner life. One self-caring step at a time, I unravel my harmful habits of behavior and the thoughts that hold them in place.

Step 4-5 Affirmation: My interior power is activated by self-awareness. I'm curious and always learning something new about myself. Within a compassionate community, I celebrate my life-affirming behaviors and accept responsibility for my ineffective behaviors. I'm committed to my transformation.

Step 6-7 Affirmation: I'm entirely ready to deepen my inner well-being. I cultivate new thoughts to inspire healthier behaviors and outcomes. My life journey is orchestrated by my own inner wisdom. I actively participate in my transformation. In the fullness of time, I'm transformed at a deeper level of my being.

Step 8-9 Affirmation: Certain that I love myself, I welcome clarity in my relationships. Having forgiven myself, I take active responsibility for the consequences of my ineffective behaviors in other people's lives.

Step 10 Affirmation: I'm present in my own life. Today I acknowledge the gifts and challenges of my life with gratitude. I celebrate my life-affirming behaviors. I take responsibility for my ineffective behaviors. I am at peace.

Step 11 Affirmation: I place myself in the stream of wisdom flowing through my life. I make conscious contact with my truest self and clearest thought. I am at home.

Step 12 Affirmation: I live in harmony with my deepest wisdom, truest self, and clearest thought. I bring truth, wisdom, and clarity into the world around me. I belong.

The journey home begins with a deep breath and the courageous vulnerability of acknowledging that we have lost our way and need guidance to find our way home. On the journey home, we are restored to peace, sanity, and a loving relationship with ourselves.

Chapter 3
A Two-Fold Acknowledgement

Step 1 as Written

We admitted we were powerless over alcohol and that our lives had become unmanageable.

Step 1 as Rewritten

Caught in the swirl of my habits of behavior, I have lost touch with myself and my life has become unmanageable. I reach out for support. This is a brave action on my own behalf.

Men and women have different experiences of the concept of power. For men to acknowledge their powerlessness means relinquishing the illusion of power in which they have been saturated since childhood. This admission allows them to seek significant connection and mutually supportive relationships within a spiritual, therapeutic, or recovery context.

On the other hand, women have been admitting powerlessness most of their lives. Our access to thrones, negotiating tables, board rooms, pulpits, and presidencies has been limited. Our position has been clear—we are inferior and our power is limited. Thus the admission of powerlessness, as defined by men, has not been woman affirming.

A woman-affirming recovery encourages us to reclaim our original power. Women redefine power as the capacity to author their own lives, act on their own behalf, handle whatever confronts them, and gather the resources necessary to heal into the present. These capacities are fostered in community.

For men, the admission of powerlessness was essential to experience connection with others. For many women, walking into their first therapy appointment, women's support group, or recovery meeting is a powerful act on their own behalf. The journey home begins with the courageous vulnerability of acknowledging that we have lost our way and need guidance to find our way home. A woman-affirming recovery affirms that vulnerability and power are partners on our journey home.

UNMANAGEABLE LIVES

In the fullness of time, we hit bottom. We become dizzy, aching, depleted, lost, sick, addicted, fed up, or bankrupt. Recognizing the unmanageability of our lives, we finally reach out for support. Unmanageability takes many forms—here are four ways it tends to manifest itself in our lives.

1. Having lost our capacity to act on our own behalf (as a result of the stupor brought about by alcohol, drugs, debt, food, or an obsessive relationship with work, child, lover, friend or co-worker) we seek help. We are limited by our habits of behavior.

    > "I sought help when I finally admitted I was powerless over work addiction, which resulted in my total isolation, the destruction of my primary relationship, and the deterioration of my health. This state of affairs led me to my first support group."

2. Having relinquished authorship of our lives, we seek help. Twisted out of shape, it made great sense to turn our lives over to lovers, jobs, causes, and religions. We are limited as a result of being estranged from our own lives.

    > "I sought help after ending a dysfunctional relationship where I allowed my life and self-esteem to slide so that I was in debt, out of work, and without friends.
    >
    > Having no grounding in a sense of self, my life spun out of control into permanent isolation. I despaired

of ever finding a firm footing from which to build a life."

3. Acknowledging our lack of resources to deal with the addiction of child, spouse, or friend, we seek help. We are limited by our lack of knowledge and resources.

    > "Faced with the alcoholism of my son, I tried to save him. I dragged the family to a program to learn about the disease. I organized family and friends to meet with an intervention counselor. I was certain I was powerful enough to get him to stop drinking. Once none of these efforts bore fruit, I came to Al-Anon."

4. Acknowledging our lack of resources to deal with the past's influence on the present, we seek help. The past's intrusion into the present may manifest as recurring childhood memories; a pattern of failed intimate relationships; or as an ever-present guilt, shame and self-destructive streak deposited in us by our early experiences. We are limited in dealing with demons that seem beyond our reach.

    > "I can't change the fact that I did not receive emotional nurturing from my parents. This resulted in my belief that I don't deserve to be loved. Since I can't expect love, nurture, and support, I never ask for help. I hide my neediness.
    >
    > When the pain becomes unbearable, I filled up the empty space inside with obsessive work, relationships, and shopping. My life is unmanageable because these things can't fill the hole. Realizing that this hole originated in my alcoholic family of origin, I reached out to others who'd discovered healing resources in Adult Children of Alcoholics."

33

With curiosity, reflect on these questions in your Self-Awareness Journal:

- Describe the "bottom" that led you to a support group, women's circle, or therapist.
- How did you experience the "bottom" in your health, finances, and relationships in your personal projects, dreams, aspirations?

A TWO-FOLD ACKNOWLEDGMENT

Ours is always a two-fold acknowledgment. Yes, we are limited and finite—and, we are powerful and gifted. We incorporate this two-fold acknowledgment into the 1st step:

1. I am limited and finite. Some things I cannot change.

I acknowledge that I am limited as a result of my habits of behavior, my alienation from myself, my lack of resources and knowledge, and my formative experiences. I admit: yes, I am limited; yes, there are things I cannot change; yes, I need support. To acknowledge my limits brings relief. The energy that is no longer needed to handle things beyond my control is transformed; it is now available to change those things I can change.

2. I am powerful and gifted. Some things I can change.

I acknowledge that I am powerful and gifted. There are things I can change: my life choices, my own moodiness, my response to the addiction of a co-worker or friend, the design of my own life. I can now focus on long-ignored creative interests, authoring my own relationships, ending energy-depleting friendships, taking responsibility for my ineffective behaviors, and choosing wellness resources and communities. Courage is available to exert, initiate, and move on my own behalf.

A Mindfulness Meditation: At the Stream of Living Water

Turn your attention inward by taking a few deep breaths. Descend into the clearing deep within the forest of your inner life. It is circled by a stream of living water. Sit quietly on the stream's bank and let go into the wise flow of life.

The stream of living water reminds us that we are limited and finite. That we cannot change some things no matter how hard we try, how desperately we want to rescue or fix, or how genuine our concern or profound our love.

Some burdens we are not meant to carry: The life choices of a loved one. The moodiness of a friend. The addiction of a co-worker. The struggle of an adolescent. The depression of a relative. The changing nature of life. The mistakes of the past. The unknowns of the future.

It is deeply wise to lay down these burdens, to let them go into the stream of living water, to release them into the wise flow of life. As you are reminded of a situation, concern, person, or relationship you cannot change, let it go into the stream, naming it in the quietness of your heart. Be relieved of burdens not yours to carry.

Breathing in: *I release* _____.
Breathing out: *Into the wise flow of life.*

As we let go of our futile attempts to change those things we cannot change, an abundance of energy is available to turn toward those things we can change. Ours is always a two-fold acknowledgment. Yes, we are limited and finite and we are powerful and gifted. There are many things we can change. The stream invites you to step into full responsibility for your life. Courage is available to exert, initiate, and move on your own behalf in your relationships, work-place, and world. Reach into the stream and receive courage to change the things you can, naming them in the privacy of your own heart.

> Breathing in: *I receive the courage to* _____.
> Breathing out: *I will act in my own behalf.*

Conclude your meditation by weaving an affirmation into the breath:

> Breathing in: *I have everything I need*
> Breathing out: *to let go of depleting thoughts and behaviors.*

> Breathing in: *I have everything I need*
> Breathing out: *to choose life-giving thoughts and behaviors.*

> Breathing in: *I have everything I need*
> Breathing out: *within the rich resources of my inner life.*

STEP 1 MINDFULNESS PRACTICE

Personalize the Step 1 based on a past situation or a current issue, using one or both of the suggested options below.

Option I: Use this Step 1 formula by filling in the blanks.

My life has become becomes unmanageable in these ways:
_____, _____ and _____.

I am limited. I do not have the necessary resources to deal with:
_____, _____ and _____.

I am powerful. I will reach out for resources to change the things I can. _____, _____ and _____.

Option II: Creatively personalize Step 1 inspired by the following examples.

Dysfunctional Society

Step 1: I can't change the fact that I was born into a society that idolizes a male god and prefers men. Its intense socialization process reinforced ineffective behaviors that do not support my life, including: deference to men, denigration of feminine qualities, and competition with women. I am exploring healing resources.

Dysfunctional Family of Origin

Step 1: I can't change the fact that I was born into a home with warring alcoholic parents. I was powerless as a child over their craziness and my life was unmanageable. I am powerless as an adult over the legacy of scars I carry in my body and life as a result of those early years. The past reaches into the present, touches my life, and moves it to the place of original pain. As an adult, I am courageously walking through the past. I celebrate my courage today.

Addictions

Step 1: I can't change the fact that I was born into an alcoholic home and that as a result, my thoughts and behaviors were shaped by my mother's helplessness and my father's violence. One of the ways I sought soothing and support was to eat compulsively. I have reached out for healing resources to walk through my past and heal into the present.

Relationships

Step 1: I can't change the twists and turns of another's life. I become arrogant and intrusive when I presume to know what's right for anyone else and when I exert effort to bring about the changes I prescribe. I celebrate my courage to look at this behavior and my willingness to move beyond it.

Intimate Relationships

Step 1: I cannot control whether my partner and I are compatible. My attempts to manipulate his attention so it turns toward me are driving us both crazy. I am frantic and overwhelmed. I have no idea if he is choosing this relationship freely. I celebrate my courage to look at this behavior and my willingness to move beyond it.

Life

Step 1: I can't change the imperfect nature of life—that things change and mistakes are made. When I attempt to change the changeless, my life becomes unmanageable, and I become depleted with no available energy to change what I can in my own life. I celebrate my desire to accept and honor life in all its trouble and beauty.

Specific Situations

Step 1: I can't change the fact that my mother has Alzheimer's disease and I cannot know if my finite body holds that tendency within it. I become overwhelmed with fear and desperation when I entertain that possibility for too long. I celebrate my capacity to be aware of and to articulate my fear and desperation.

Caught in the swirl of my habits of behavior,
I have lost touch with myself and my life has
become unmanageable. I reach out for support.
This is a brave action on my own behalf.

Chapter 4
Bring Many Names

Step 2 as Written

We came to believe that a power greater than ourselves can restore us to sanity.

Step 2 as Rewritten

I have come to believe in the deep wisdom of my own inner life. I stop flailing and am restored to the sanity of a loving and respectful relationship with myself.

Overwhelmed by our own addiction or caught up in the addiction of another, many of us reached out to some version of the traditional Twelve Step community for assistance. The first step "We admitted we were powerless over alcohol that our lives had become unmanageable," was relatively easy for us to acknowledge. It was the unmanageability of our lives that prompted us to seek out a community of support.

The second step "We came to believe that a power greater than ourselves could restore us to sanity" was harder to accept. Old time members spoke of "coming to believe" in a god or higher power. This "god talk" triggered our early attitudes, beliefs, and experiences with religion. Images of confessionals and Days of Atonement, pangs of guilt and shame, and the judgmental voices of rabbis and priests welled up within us.

Yet we desperately needed the support of the program so some of us twisted our sense of the divine into acceptable shapes. We stuffed the religious images of childhood back into the closets of our memory, hoping to quiet the pangs of guilt and the judgmental voices of old. We thought by ignoring our religious past, we would eventually come to believe in the god espoused by the Program. Some of us left the program unable to get the god-part.

> "When I entered Adult Children of Alcoholics and read the second step, it reminded me of the Catholic old father god in the clouds with the long white beard and his book of judgment. This image made me uncomfortable."

> "My response to the 'god-talk' of the program was mixed. One part of me was relieved that I could rely on a power greater than myself. The other part of me was embarrassed to hear members speak of Christianity's god because the image of a male god didn't comfort me as a child."

Central to the practice of the Twelve Step program, however, is the importance of choosing one's own concept of "higher power." Both AA and Al-Anon give us the permission to name the god of our understanding in whatever way is helpful to us.

> "Much to our relief we discovered we did not need to consider another's conception of God... our own was sufficient to effect contact." (The Big Book)

> "It was left entirely up to us what the name of God meant to us personally. We might have imagined God as a ruler or judge or as the quality of Universal Love, revealing itself in our lives. To some it might have been a personal God powerful, but separate from us, while to others, God might have been thought of as an essential part of all creativity." (Al-Anon's 12 Steps and 12 Traditions)

There has always been a voice in the recovery community affirming a universal spirituality and wisdom beyond gender. A search through the Big Book of AA uncovered the following inclusive images. Respond to each image through writing or drawing. Incorporate them into your prayer and meditation today.

- Universal Mind, Spirit of Nature, Spirit of the Universe (p. 12)
- All Powerful, Guiding, and Creative Intelligence (p. 49)
- Great Reality Deep Down Within Us (p. 55)
- The Mighty Purpose and Rhythm That Underlies All (p. 55)
- Presence of Infinite Power and Love (p. 56)

Although Bill Wilson's (one of the founders of AA) description of his spiritual awakening was eventually reduced to Christian constructs, its original expression did not contain traditional religious language. Reflect on the images he used to describe his spiritual awakening. Respond to them in writing or drawing:

> "The room lit up with a great white light. I was caught into an ecstasy which no words can describe. It seemed to me that I was on a mountain, and a wind, not of air but of spirit, was blowing. And then it burst on me that I was a free man. Slowly the ecstasy subsided. For a time, I was in a new world of consciousness. All about and through me was a wonderful feeling of Presence."

RECLAIMING YOUR ORIGINAL SPIRITUALITY

In the very beginning of her life, the girl-child has direct access to the spirit of life. It is as near to her as the breath that fills her. And it connects her to everything. She is not alone. Her spirit is one with the spirit of her beloved grandmother, her favorite rock, tree, and star. She develops her own methods for contacting the spirit in all things.

She climbs a tree and sits in its branches, listening. She loves the woods and listens there too. She has a special friend—a rock. She gives it a name and eats her lunch with it whenever she can. She keeps the window open next to her bed even on the coldest of nights. She loves the fresh air on her face. She pulls the covers tight around her chin and listens to the mysterious night sky. She believes that her grandmother is present even though everyone else says she is dead. Each night, she drapes the curtain over her shoulders for privacy, looks out the window near her bed, listens for Grandma and then says silent prayers to her.

Her imagination is free for a time. She does not need priest or teacher to describe god to her. Spirit erupts spontaneously in colorful and unique expressions. God is Grandma, the twinkling evening star, the gentle breeze that washes across her face, the peaceful quiet darkness after everyone has fallen asleep, and all the colors of the rainbow. And because she is a girl, her experience and expression of spirit is uniquely feminine. The spirit of the universe pulsates through her. She is full of herself.

Eventually the girl-child will turn away from the Spirit-filled One. Her original spirituality will become confined within the acceptable lines of religion. She will be taught the right way to imagine and name god. "He" will be mediated to her through words, images, stories, and myths shaped, written, and spoken by men. She will adopt the god she is given. It is too dangerous to rebel. If she dares to venture out of the lines by communing with the spirit of a tree, the mysterious night sky, or her grandma, she will be labeled heretic, backslide, or witch. She is told:

> Prideful One, your grandma is not god; neither is your favorite star or rock. God has only one name and face. You shall have no gods before him. God is Father, Son, and Holy Ghost. He is found in the church, heavens, and holy book, not in you. God is the god of the fathers and sons; the daughters have no say in the matter. As it was in the beginning, it is now and ever shall be.

The Spirit-Filled One falls asleep. Occasionally she awakens to remind the girl-child-turned-woman of what she once knew. These periodic reminders are painful. The woman fills her life with

42

distractions so she will not hear the quiet inner voice, calling her to return home. Years later, new teachers enter the woman's life —a therapist, a self-help group, a support circle, a beloved friend, or perhaps this book. They remind her of what she once knew:

> *Spirit-filled One, your grandma is god and so are your favorite star and rock. God has many names and many faces. God is Mother, Daughter, and Wise Old Crone. She is found in your mothers, in your daughters, and in you. She is Mother of all Living and blessed are her daughters. You are girl-woman made in her image. The spirit of the universe pulsates through you.*

Women are reclaiming the divine feminine today. Surrounded by women from every age and inspired by their courage, we are committing the forbidden acts of naming and imagining the gods of our understanding as Goddess, Woman God, and God the Mother. Although we are not all devotees of the goddess, it was essential for us to extend our historical and theological vision to include the divine feminine.

Some find "her" within traditional religion in the images and stories of Eve and Mary, Sophia and Shekinah, Miriam and Esther, Naomi and Ruth, Tamar and Susanna, and of countless unnamed women. They are incorporating these women's stories into their liturgies and prayers. Others find her on the margins of patriarchal history in the images and stories of the Goddess. They're incorporating her images into their paintings and songs, altars and prayers, and they're weaving her ancient festivals and beliefs into their unfolding spirituality.

Inspired by a view of history that reaches beyond the beginning defined by men, women are assuming theological equality with religious traditions and reclaiming the richness of their own imaginations. We have come to believe that the theological tasks performed by men throughout the ages were not inspired by a god out there somewhere. Rather they were prompted by a very human inclination to answer existential questions and order disparate experiences into a coherent whole through religious imagination.

Humankind's religious imagination has always given birth to goddesses and gods, and to stories that attempt to make sense of our beginnings and endings. No longer held hostage by a truncated view of history or by the dominance of the Genesis account of creation, our imaginations are once again free.

THE CHANGING FACE OF GOD

As face of god changes in our experience, we bring our own images of the divine to the Steps. In the spirit of AA's founding principle, we reclaim our right to name and imagine the god of our understanding. These woman-affirming principles inform our "coming to believe" process:

- The Ultimate truth, wisdom, and power of the universe is far deeper, higher, wider and richer than any name or image we use to refer to it. Every name and image must be held loosely. Mystery cannot be confined in our names and images.

- Every name and image has limitations. The wounding of women as a result of the dominance of male god language must be taken into account. A time may come when a particular image is no longer useful. The wisdom of your inner process will provide another image that is more helpful. Honor the changing face of god in your life.

A Mindfulness Meditation: Bring Many Names

The ultimate truth, wisdom, and mystery of the Universe is far deeper, higher, wider, and richer than any name or image we use to refer to it. Mystery cannot be confined within a language. Bring many names... and no names at all.

Bring many names... moving us beyond the limitations of gender:

> Breathing in: *Deeper Wisdom*
> > Breathing out: *Source of Life*
>
> Breathing in: *Community of Support*
> > Breathing out: *Sacred Breath*

Bring many names... retaining the relational quality of the divine:

> Breathing in: *Loving Wise One*
> > Breathing out: *Welcoming Friend*
>
> Breathing in: *Compassionate One*
> > Breathing out: *Nurturing One*

Bring many names... weaving traditional names into an unfolding spirituality:

> Breathing in: *Loving Father*
> > Breathing out: *Abba*
>
> Breathing in: *Wise Spirit*
> > Breathing out: *Mother-Father God*

Bring many names... challenging the idolatry of traditional religion:

> Breathing in: *Goddess.*
> > Breathing out: *Woman God*
>
> Breathing in: *Sister God*
> > Breathing out: *Sophia*
>
> Breathing in: *Big Mama*
> > Breathing out: *Mother of All Living*

Bring many names and no names at all. In the silence. leave space for the unknown.

> Breathing in: *In the silence,*
> > Breathing out: *I leave space for the unknown.*

Women's Stories

Notice your reaction to the following ways women have personalized Step 2.

> "I have come to believe in a Sister God who stands beside me, offering support and gentle guidance. She is a peer rather than a power distant or apart from me. She supports me as I make the choices that shape my life. She restores me to serenity."

> "I imagine Higher Power as the power at work in me and in everyone throughout the universe. I can let go into this source of empowerment. In doing so, I am not surrendering; rather, I am choosing life."

> "I have come to believe in myself. I know that the voices of negativity and derision are my family's voice, not my own. I believe at the very depth of me is the truth of my life. I am restored to a quietness in which my truth makes itself known to me."

RESTORED TO SANITY

Imagine being restored to financial solvency, healthy eating, abstinence from drugs and alcohol. Imagine being restored to serenity and joy, and to the ability to create art, express your feelings, and choose healthy relationships. Until we imagine something, it remains an impossibility. Once imagined, it becomes our experience. Imagination is essential to our transformational journey. Be inspired by Lydia's vision of sanity:

> "I am available to myself. The shadows have dissolved as the bright good light penetrates. I develop a good vocation and am financially responsible. I recover the abandoned pieces of myself, the bits of feeling, humor, anger, grief, sexuality that I had disowned. As my dynamic feelings become more available to me, my creativity broadens and

informs my work and relationships. I meet others with less judgment and more kindness. I become attentive to my own needs. I sleep. I enjoy handling and eating the lovely stuff of the earth."

Imagine what sanity would look like in your particular situation. Use the following process to compose your own vision of hope:

- Acknowledge the injury to be healed.
  Describe what healing looks, feels, tastes, and sounds like.
- Acknowledge the ineffective behavior to be transformed.
  Describe what the new behavior looks, feels, tastes, and sounds like.
- Acknowledge the obsessive patterns of thought or action to be transformed.
  Describe what freedom from obsession looks, feels, tastes, and sounds like.
- Acknowledge the depleting relationship to be relinquished.
  Describe what life-enhancing relationships look, feel, taste, and sound like.
- Acknowledge the damaging messages to be exorcised.
  Describe what life-affirming messages look, feel, taste, and sound like.

MINDFULNESS PRACTICE: STEP 2

Personalize Step 2 using one or both of the suggested options. Continue with the same issue used in Step 1 or choose a new one.

Option 1: Use this simple Step 2 formula.

I have come to believe that (describe what you've come to believe) will restore me to (describe what "sanity" looks like in your specific situation).

Option 2: Work Step 2 inspired by the creative personalizations that follow.

Dysfunctional Society

Step 1: I cannot change the fact that I was born into a society that idolizes a male god and prefers men. Its intense socialization process reinforced ineffective behaviors that do not support my life, including: deference to men, denigration of feminine qualities, and competition with women. I am exploring healing resources.

Step 2: I have come to believe that Deeper Wisdom resides within me, reaching beneath my ineffective behaviors. This deeper wisdom restores me to my original power—I no longer defer to men. It restores me to my original connection—I celebrate women. It restores me to my original goodness—I embrace the rich resources within me.

Dysfunctional Family of Origin

Step 1: I cannot change the fact that I was born into a home with warring alcoholic parents. I was powerless as a child over their craziness and my life was unmanageable. I am powerless as an adult over the legacy of scars I carry in my body and life as a result of those early years. The past reaches into the present, touches my life, and moves it to the place of original pain. As an adult, I am walking through the past. I celebrate my courage today.

Step 2: I have come to trust that Deeper Wisdom holds my life and has been faithful to me since childhood. I have always found a way to thrive in life. I have made a choice to live that is deep and abiding. I say it's fragile, but I'm seeing how tenacious it truly is.

Addictions

Step 1: I cannot change the fact that I was born into an alcoholic home and that as a result, my thoughts and behaviors were shaped by my mother's helplessness and my father's violence. One of the ways I sought soothing and support was to eat compulsively. I have reached out for healing resources to walk through my past and heal into the present.

Step 2: I believe my deepest impulse is toward life and health. I'm restored to a loving relationship with my body. I listen to its needs and meet them in a self-caring way.

Relationships

Step 1: I cannot change the twists and turns of another's life. I become arrogant and intrusive when I presume to know what's right for anyone else and when I exert effort to bring about the changes I prescribe. I celebrate my willingness to look at and move beyond this behavior.

Step 2: I have come to believe that a deeper wisdom is at work in his / her life and in my own. Deeper Wisdom will remind me of the way home to myself. It restores me to serenity and respect for each person's sacred journey.

Intimate Relationships

Step 1: I cannot control whether my partner and I are compatible. My attempts to manipulate so his attention turns toward me are driving us both crazy. I am frantic and overwhelmed. I have no idea if he is choosing this relationship freely. I celebrate my willingness to look at this behavior and to move beyond it.

Step 2: I believe that relationships unfold according to the deep wisdom of attraction, compatibility, and intention. I trust and listen for this inherent wisdom.

Life

Step 1: I cannot change the imperfect nature of life—that things change, that mistakes are made. When I attempt to change the changeless, my life becomes unmanageable, and I become frustrated and depleted with no available energy to change what I can in my life. I celebrate my desire to accept and honor life in all its trouble and beauty, gift and challenge.

Step 2: I have come to believe that a deep wisdom reaches beneath the changing nature of life and that my own life unfolds according to its design. I am restored to trust in this organic unfolding.

Specific Situations

Step 1: I am powerless over my mother's Alzheimer's disease and whether my finite body will develop the same disease. I become overwhelmed with fear when I entertain that possibility. I celebrate my capacity to articulate my fear and desperation.

Step 2: I have come to believe that my life is held by a deep wisdom that will restore me to the sanity of living this day... fully and completely.

I have come to believe in the deep wisdom of my own inner life.
I stop flailing and am restored to the sanity of a loving
and respectful relationship with myself.

Chapter 5

Restored to Wholeness

Step 3 as Written

Made a decision to turn our life and will over to the care of God as we understood God.

Step 3 as Rewritten

I turn my current situation over to the deep wisdom that flows in and through my life. One self-caring step at a time, I unravel my harmful habits of behavior and the thoughts that hold them in place.

Sitting in a Twelve Step meeting several years ago, I listened as a woman spoke about learning to trust the god of her understanding: "When I let Higher Power take charge, everything works out fine. When I'm in the driver's seat, I blow it every time." Inspired by her talk, several other women acknowledged that they were fundamentally ill-equipped to deal with life. Based on their sense of inadequacy, each one found it necessary to "surrender" to a power greater than themselves.

Later that week I sat in a women's support circle as a woman complained about the unavailability of her therapist who was on vacation: "I have to see her every week or things begin to fall apart around me. I don't seem to have what it takes to live my life without the assistance of a trained professional."

While on the book tour supporting *A God Who Looks Like Me*, I was interviewed on a religious radio show. During the call-in part of the program, the inevitable question about sin and salvation was asked: "Do you believe we are sinners and in need of the salvation God offers?" I told the caller that my own inner wisdom was trustworthy and that it was communicated to me through my natural impulses, instincts, and intuition. I no longer needed the salvation offered by gods, higher powers, therapists, or gurus. The caller was appalled. "We can't trust ourselves," she exclaimed, "we are sinful and left to our own devices, we will mess things up every time. God is the only trustworthy one."

Convinced that our lives are not our own, we become alienated from our inner sense of what is true and appropriate for us. We become experts at watching the way others live and we shape our lives accordingly. From talk show hosts, to therapists and trainers, to the countless apps and experts we consult to design our experience, everyone knows better than we do.

Consequently, we have spent lifetimes trying to fit into someone else's idea of what is right for us: assembling our bodies according to society's formula of the perfect woman, forming our thoughts and opinions to suit the audience, limiting our feelings to what's acceptable, and formulating our behavior and actions according to the expectations of others. We have become emotionally crippled as a result of habitually abandoning ourselves into the shapes of others. Each surrender of our feelings, truth, and originality becomes a mini-abdication of who we are.

The central virtue in a shame-based expression of recovery is obedience to a power greater than ourselves. Being asked by the third step to turn our will and lives over to a Higher Power continues the disempowering process that alienates us from our own resources and our own powers of self-assertion and determination.

EMBRACING DEEPER WISDOM

Reminded of the truth about ourselves, we embrace a woman-affirming recovery that reminds us of our original willfulness. We remember ancient women who valued their willfulness and encouraged their daughters to believe their "will" was valid and achievable in the world. We remember ancient ways that taught women to refuse submission and subordination, and applauded women for exerting, initiating, and moving on their own behalf in harmony with their own deep wisdom.

Inspired by the stories of old, women are turning inward—instead of looking to a god or higher power outside of our lives for salvation, we journey "home" to ourselves. Instead of ascending to enlightened states of being that involve the denial of the self, we have discovered that ours is a journey of descent: we look deep within to reclaim forgotten aspects of ourselves.

In our descent, many of us rediscover "Sophia," which is the Greek word for wisdom. She is a feminine aspect of the divine found in the Hebrew Scriptures. Her presence in the male pantheon of gods has been obscured, but not completely eradicated. In the Gnostic writings, considered heretical by the "orthodox" church, Sophia was present at creation and escorted Adam and Eve toward self-awareness.

Women are reclaiming Sophia as a representation of their own inner wisdom. No longer is "god's will" imposed from outside of their lives—wisdom unfolds from within them and is in sync with their own natural gifts and capacities. No longer available to turn their lives and wills over to gods, gurus, and experts, they're refusing to surrender except to Wisdom's urgings. No longer abdicating responsibility for their lives, they are employing their own willfulness in harmony with Wisdom's ways.

A Mindfulness Meditation: An Encounter with Deeper Wisdom
The use of "deeper" in the book's title acknowledges that a woman's journey is one of descent. Instead of looking to a god or higher power outside of our lives, we look deep within to reclaim forgotten aspects of ourselves. The use of "wisdom" acknowledges that in our descent we rediscover the original wisdom that orchestrated our days and development in the very

beginning of life. Deeper Wisdom restores us to wholeness and to a loving relationship with ourselves and others.

Wisdom resides in the depths of us below the turbulence of our mind's activity and the fluctuations of daily living. She pre-dates our socialization by religion, society, and family. She is available to us in the stillness. She is trustworthy and the one to whom we open in prayer/reflection/contemplation. Experiment with the following meditation to improve your conscious contact with Wisdom.

Turn your attention inward by taking a few deep breaths. Imagine standing in the clearing deep within the forest of your being. You are surrounded by ancient redwoods. Everything breathes in the forest.

> Breathing in... *I savor the breath of life*
> Breathing out... *As it flows in and through and around me.*

A circle of benches appears. Sit on one of the benches. You are waiting for Wisdom to arrive. She may appear as someone you know: a wise teacher, grandmother, sister, or friend. Or Wisdom may visit as a mythic figure: the Wise Old Woman, Mother of all Living, Goddess, or the Divine Girl-Child.

In the fullness of time, Wisdom walks into the circle and sits across from you. Her eyes invite you to speak: "Tell me about the confusing situation, troubling relationship, disturbing memory, or current life challenge consuming your thoughts." In the stillness, describe your life challenge in your imagination or in your Self Awareness Journal (SAJ).

In the stillness following your response to her, ask Wisdom to answer a specific question about the situation you described or to offer a creative strategy for addressing your challenge. If an image forms, draw it. If a message wells up, write it down. Do not edit what comes. Simply write it down. When finished with your dialogue, weave an affirmation into the breath:

Breathing in... *I come home to the rich resources of my inner wisdom.*
Breathing out... *Home is always waiting.*

TURNING IT OVER

"Turning it over" is the shorthand used at 12 Step meetings for the surrender called for in the third step. In a woman-affirming recovery we redefine "turning it over" to include a whole new set of possibilities. Most of them involve getting out of our heads and finding the path to our hearts and Deeper Wisdom. Add your own alternatives to the list below and practice them this week.

- We no longer attack our problems. We turn them over to the silence of prayer and meditation and listen for the voice of our Deeper Wisdom.

- Imagining her concern as a pancake, Jen flips it over to see it from a different perspective and to consider a whole new set of options for dealing with it.

- We turn the problem over to the wisdom of our support group or women's spirituality circle by going to a meeting and talking about it.

- We turn the difficulty over by talking to a wise friend. We invite her to support us in discovering the inner resources available to confront the situation.

My favorite passage in Alanon's *One Day at a Time* book of daily readings is this Ralph Waldo Emerson quotation that offers us another "turning it over" practice: "There's guidance for each of us, and by lowly listening, we shall hear the right word. Place yourself in the middle of the stream of power and wisdom, which flows into your life. Then without effort, you are impelled to truth and perfect contentment."

Emerson affirms that wisdom and power reside within us. Our only action is to stand in the middle of the stream flowing through our lives. Using this image, Step 2 and 3 would read: "I have come to believe that a deep stream of wisdom and power flows into and through my life. Without effort, it restores me to wholeness and deepening contentment and satisfaction. Daily, I place myself in this stream."

How do you place yourself in the middle of the stream of power and wisdom, flowing in and through your life? Add your responses to the ones below:

> *I let go of the outcome, allowing the stream to flow unencumbered.*

> *I place myself in the stream by reducing the number of activities I engage in and by making it okay to be quiet and listen.*

> *I go to meetings. This is turning my life over to the Deeper Wisdom of the program. I allow what I hear to influence my dilemmas and life-challenges.*

> *I choose to be myself with no judgment and blame. I choose to unconditionally love myself. In the past, the stream has been cluttered with the debris of self-judgment.*

> *I place myself in the stream by reading spiritual books, attending lectures, and listening to speakers who teach me new ways of responding to familiar situations.*

> *When stuck in the familiar ways, I place myself in the babbling brook. I am refreshed. Unwanted anxieties flow away downstream. I am restored to harmony.*

STEP 3 MINDFULNESS PRACTICE

Your Step 2 belief will shape the decisions you make in Step 3. For example:

- If you've come to believe in a community of support (Step 2), you will choose to spend time in that community to receive its healing resources (Step 3).

- If you have come to believe that intuition is your guiding light (Step 2), you will develop ways of listening to intuition and acting on its guidance (Step 3).

Personalize Step 3 based on what you have come to believe using the suggested options below. Continue with the same issue used in Steps 1-2 or choose a new one.

Option 1: Personalize one of the following Step 3 templates.

I choose to 'turn it over' to _____
(describe the god of your understanding) by _____,
_____ and _____.

I place myself in the middle of the stream of wisdom and power that flows through my life by _____,
_____ and _____.

I have made the following healthy decisions: _____,
_____ and _____.

Option 2: Work the Step inspired by the personalizations below.

Dysfunctional Society

Step 1: I cannot change the fact that I was born into a society that idolizes a male god and prefers men. Its intense socialization process reinforced ineffective behaviors that do not support my life, including: deference to men, denigration of feminine qualities, and competition with women. I am exploring healing resources.

Step 2: I have come to believe that Deeper Wisdom resides within me, reaching beneath my ineffective behaviors. This deeper wisdom restores me to my original power—I no longer defer to men. It restores me to my original connection—I celebrate women. It restores me to my original goodness—I embrace the rich resources within me.

Step 3: I turn toward healing resources to restore me to wholeness and to, one day at a time, choose life affirming behaviors that support my recovery and life: I no longer defer to men. I celebrate women. I embrace the rich resources within me.

Dysfunctional Family of Origin

Step 1: I cannot change the fact that I was born into a home with warring alcoholic parents. As a child I was powerless over their craziness and my life was unmanageable. I am powerless as an adult over the legacy of scars I carry in my body and life as a result of those early years. The past reaches into the present, touches my life, and moves it to the place of original pain. I am courageously walking through the past. I celebrate my courage today.

Step 2: I have come to trust that Deeper Wisdom holds my life and has been faithful to me since childhood. I have always found a way to thrive in life. I have made a choice to live that is deep and abiding. I say it's fragile, but I'm seeing how tenacious it truly is.

Step 3: I choose to create support systems to hold me as memories are brought to surface and as thoughts and ineffective behaviors are triggered. I spend time each week in a supportive community to hear its healing words and learn its tools of support. I now have the life skills to face anything that comes along. I am no longer powerless. I am learning new ways of being, thinking, acting, and expressing feelings.

Addictions

Step 1: I cannot change the fact that I was born into an alcoholic home and that as a result, my thoughts and behaviors were shaped by my mother's helplessness and my father's violence. One of the ways I sought soothing and support was to eat compulsively. I have reached out for healing resources to walk through my past and heal into the present.

Step 2: I believe my deepest impulse is toward life and health. I'm restored to a loving relationship with my body. I listen to its needs and meet them in a self-caring way.

Step 3: I spend time in a community of support weekly. There I am reminded of the tools of support available to empower me to feel my feelings and show up for my life. I am creating a safe home in which I feed myself nurturing meals.

Relationships

Step 1: I cannot change the twists and turns of another's life. I become arrogant and intrusive when I presume to know what's right for anyone else and when I exert effort to bring about the changes I prescribe. I celebrate my willingness to look at and move beyond this behavior.

Step 2: I have come to believe that a deeper wisdom is at work in his/her life and in my own. Deeper Wisdom will remind me of the way home to myself. It restores my serenity and respect for each person's sacred journey.

Step 3: I turn _____ over to the wisdom of his/her own process. I will not intrude. Theirs is a sacred journey. Across the distance, I honor and respect _____'s sacred journey.

Intimate Relationships

Step 1: I cannot control whether my partner and I are compatible. My attempts to manipulate his attention so it turns toward me are driving us both crazy. I am frantic and overwhelmed. I have no idea if he is choosing this relationship freely. I celebrate my willingness to look at and move beyond this behavior.

Step 2: I believe that relationships unfold according to the deep wisdom of attraction, compatibility, and intention. I trust and listen for this inherent wisdom.

Step 3: I turn my script of the way the relationship should unfold over to the deeper wisdom. I spend my time listening to this wise inner voice. I let go of the outcome.

Life

Step 1: I cannot change the imperfect nature of life—that things change and mistakes are made. When I attempt to change the changeless, my life becomes unmanageable and I become frustrated and depleted with no time or energy to change what I can in my own life. I celebrate my desire to accept and honor life in all its trouble and beauty, gift and challenge.

Step 2: I have come to believe that a deep wisdom reaches beneath the changing nature of life and that my own life unfolds according to its design. I trust in this organic unfolding.

Step 3: I choose to accept life as it is, with its bursts of light, unpredictability, and surprise. I choose to be grateful for the beauty of life just as it is. I choose to acknowledge my gratitude for life with my sponsor and at my meetings.

Specific Situations

Step 1: I am powerless over my mother's Alzheimer's disease and whether my finite body will develop the same disease. I become overwhelmed with fear when I entertain that possibility for too long. I celebrate my capacity to articulate my fear and desperation.

Step 2: I have come to believe that my life is held by a deep wisdom that will restore me to the sanity of living this day... fully and completely.

Step 3: I turn my future over to the faithful stream of wisdom, flowing through my life. Without effort, I flow toward truth and perfect contentment one day at a time.

I turn my current situation over to the deep wisdom that flows in and through my life. One self-caring step at a time, I unravel my harmful habits of behavior and the thoughts that hold them in place.

Chapter 6

The ADW Three-Step: Letting Go of Over-Responsibility

Step 1: I am not responsible for the swirling thoughts, feelings, behaviors and actions of others. I become dizzy when I step into anyone's swirl.

Step 2: I have come to believe that Deeper Wisdom is at work in their lives. Deeper Wisdom restores me to the serenity of my own life and reminds me of the way home.

Step 3: I turn others over to the wisdom of their own life-process. I will not violate their intellectual, spiritual, and emotional boundaries. Across the distance, I choose to honor and respect their sacred journeys.

As I mentioned in Chapter 1, in the very beginning of your life, you were acquainted with the exquisite natural resources of your breath, body, and inner life. You breathed deeply into your belly. You loved your body. You were in touch with the wisdom within your own life. Over time, however, the girl-child becomes disconnected from the "home" within her. She learns three ineffective, yet culturally mandated, behaviors.

1. Over-Responsibility: The girl-child is encouraged to get caught up in the actions, thoughts, feelings, and journeys of others. As a result, she assumes inappropriate responsibility for the cause, modification, and outcome of the choices, behaviors, and actions of others. Distracted, we lose touch with our own lives.

2. People-Pleasing: The girl-child is encouraged to shape her body, thoughts, feelings, behaviors, and relationships according to the specifications of others. As a result, she develops a crippling over-sensitivity to and dependence on

the opinions of others. Twisted out of shape, we lose touch with our inner resources of wisdom and creativity.

3. Over-Involvement: The girl-child is groomed to be a caretaker. She will be expected to anticipate and then meet the emotional and physical needs of others. As a result, she becomes preoccupied with servicing others with her energy, attention, and creativity. Depleted, we lose touch with our own needs and desires.

Caught in the swirls of others, twisted into the shapes of others, and depleted by the demands of others, she becomes outer-directed and loses touch with herself. Estranged from her own life, she becomes susceptible to the swirls of others.

A swirl is any relationship or person; religion, cause, or dogma; food or drug; activity or project outside of oneself that becomes the controlling or organizing focus of one's time, energy, and attention. Women's "swirls" range from pleasing boyfriends / girlfriends to rescuing alcoholic children, from supporting partners' careers to meeting the body-beautiful demands of the culture, from addictions to compulsive distractions, and from searching for the "perfect" self-improvement regimen to fulfilling the expectations of new age gurus.

Swirling requires disengagement from our bodies—we ignore our organic needs; from our breath—being out of breath with no time to catch our breath; and from our inner life— being out of touch with ourselves and not knowing what's really going on.
And yet our swirling doesn't stop until we are ready.

Swirls have a life and purpose of their own. They are held within a trustworthy process. We swirl until we lose our breath and bearings, until we become dizzy. Unable to eat or sleep, fragile and shaking, we become willing to journey home to ourselves and take full responsibility for our own lives and awesome potential.

Hannah describes her swirls:

> "My primary swirl has been trying to manage other people's lives. At the end of college, instead of getting my life ready for my own future, I took on my first husband as my fix-it cause. I encouraged him to get a job, found him an apartment, and helped him apply to college.
>
> After the breakup of that marriage, I stopped swirling for a while. I got in a camper and traveled with my dog for two years. I rediscovered my spiritual center. I was at home with myself. But I didn't know how to bring that peace with me when I re-entered a relationship. It didn't take long to get caught in another rescuing swirl.
>
> I was truly dizzy and my life was out of balance when I joined a woman's circle. I was fearful for my alcoholic son's life. I couldn't sleep and I cried a lot. I kept trying to figure out a solution to hand him. After months of panic, it dawned on me that I wasn't handling my own life. By swirling in his, I was jeopardizing my own health, sanity, friendships, and professional commitments."

THE ADW THREE STEP

The ADW Three Step supports us to disengage from the swirls of others and become grounded in our own lives. The first three steps have been reframed to apply to our tendency to swirl outside of our own lives. This over-involvement and over-responsibility plagues many of us and depletes our life-energy. Practice the ADW Three Step daily until it becomes deeply embedded within your relationships.

Step 1: I am not responsible for the swirling thoughts, feelings, behaviors, and actions of others. I become dizzy when I step into their swirls.

> Step 1 reminds us that we are limited and finite, that there are some things we cannot change no matter how hard we try; no matter how desperately we want to rescue, fix, or work things out; no matter how genuine our concern or profound our love. It also reminds us of the organic consequences of stepping into the swirls of others—we become dizzy.
>
> Personalize Step 1 by naming the particular person, describing the nature of their swirls, and outlining the ways you become dizzy: "I am not responsible for the swirling thoughts, feelings, behaviors, and actions of _____. I become dizzy when I step into his/her swirls by _____, _____, and _____."

Step 2: I have come to believe that there is a Deeper Wisdom at work in his/her life and in my own. The Deeper Wisdom restores me to the serenity of my own life.

> Step 2 invites us to remember the god of our understanding. Our journey has been one of descent. We have looked deep within to reclaim forgotten aspects of ourselves and to rediscover the wisdom that orchestrated our days and development in the very beginning of life. This Deeper Wisdom restores us to wholeness and to respectful relationships, with ourselves and others.
>
> Personalize Step 2 by naming the swirl and using metaphors in harmony with your own beliefs: "I have come to believe a Deeper Wisdom/God/Goddess is at work in _____'s life and in my own. Deeper Wisdom/God/Goddess reminds me of the way home and restores me to serenity of my own life."

Step 3: I turn _____ over to the wisdom of their own process. I will not violate their intellectual and emotional boundaries. Across the distance, I honor their journey.

> Step 3 invites us to take responsibility for the ways we have trespassed the lives of others. When we get caught up in their swirls, we assume we know what's best for them and orchestrate interventions based on our own anxiety.

> Step 3 invites us to "turn them over" to a wisdom deeper than yours and to choose not to intrude into someone else's life-process, recognizing the impossibility of knowing what is truest and best for another person.

> Step 3 invites us to accept that infinite distances exist between even the closest human beings. It invites us to love the distance by seeing the "other" whole against a wide-open sky! (Rilke)

> Personalize the Step: "I turn _____ over to the Wisdom of his/her own process. I will not violate _____'s intellectual, spiritual, emotional boundaries. Across the distance, I choose to honor and respect _____'s sacred journey."

MINDFULNESS PRACTICE: STEPS 1-2-3

Are you caught in the swirl of pleasing your girlfriend/boyfriend, rescuing your adult children, supporting your partner's career, meeting the body-beautiful demands of the culture, searching for the "perfect" self-improvement regimen, or fulfilling the expectations of a new age philosophy or guru? Are you whirling in chaos not your own, losing touch with your breath and body, and the grounding center within you?

Befriend the richness within you by reclaiming your natural resources. Redirect your energy away from the "swirling" patterns of old toward adventures of self-discovery. Recognize each impulse to step into the life of another as a disconnection from yourself. Learn to pause, notice the disconnection without judgment, and then return home, making conscious contact with your breath, woman-body, and inner life. Allow Hannah's example to inspire you to release and let go:

Step 1: I'm not responsible for the swirling feelings and actions of my alcoholic son. I become exhausted when I step into his swirls to try to rescue him. I neglect work responsibilities because he consumes my thoughts and time.

Step 2: I have come to believe that a deeper wisdom is at work in his life and in my own. He will find his own way in the fullness of time. Wisdom will restore me to the serenity of my own life and will remind me of the way home to myself and to the fulfillment of my own personal responsibilities.

Step 3: I turn my son over to the wisdom of his process. Across the distance, I honor and respect his sacred journey. I will not violate his boundaries by opening his mail, listening to his conversations, or monitoring his money.

Women's Stories

Janet: I do not have the time or energy to get caught up in the swirls of my past. My current life demands my energy. I do not need to resolve every unpleasant occurrence of my past before I can choose to live in the present. Whenever I begin to obsess about my past life, I will re-establish conscious contact with my breath and body, and the grounding center within me and then work on a self-enriching project:

- Centering on my breath.
- Playing in my garden.
- Taking the time to read.
- Spending time with my creative projects.

Renee: I do not have the energy to focus my thoughts, time, and energy on my ex-lover. This depletes the energy I need to take to care of myself. His life is none of my business. Whenever I begin to get caught up in his life, I will re-establish conscious contact with the grounding center within me and work on a self-enriching project:

- The launch of a fitness program that includes daily walk-runs and yoga.
- The development of my career and forward movement toward my financial goals.
- Relating responsibly to my widening circle of friends.

Karen: I will not be diverted from the projects in my life by making senseless comparisons between my life and those of my friends and associates. If others have something in their lives that I want and can reasonably attain, I will act to get it for myself rather than feeling victimized. When I'm tempted to get caught up in the swirl of useless comparisons, I'll turn toward a self-enriching project:

- Increasing the number of social contacts in my life;
- Taking the risk to sign up for a ceramics class;
- Putting in regular work on my dissertation topic.

When we are caught up in the swirls of others, they become a burden to us. When we are settled and grounded in the serenity and responsibility of our own lives, we are free to support others in ways that enhance them and do not dizzy or burden us.

Chapter 7
Merciful Consciousness

Steps 4 and 5 as Written

Made a searching and fearless moral inventory of ourselves. Admitted to God, to ourselves, and to another human being the exact nature of our wrongs.

Steps 4 and 5 as Rewritten

Turning a merciful eye toward myself, I inventory both my life-affirming and ineffective behaviors, and identify the habits of thought that inspire them. In the company of trustworthy people, I celebrate my life-affirming behaviors, accept responsibility for my ineffective behaviors, and make a commitment to my transformation.

The fourth step invite us to come out of denial. We are encouraged to turn our awareness toward ourselves. We have been released from shame and self-rejection. Certain that we love ourselves, we welcome awareness and honesty. Our awareness of ourselves is informed by self-love and tenderness. It embraces the two-fold nature of our lives, our incredible goodness and our vulnerable humanness.

A fourth step inventory must always include a celebration of our goodness and a recognition of the origins of our ineffective behaviors along with an acceptance of responsibility for them. In one sense, the process of recovery is a continuous and fluid fourth step. From this point of view, we reframe the key words used in the original version of Steps 4 and 5:

Searching: We have begun the descent into the richness of our inner lives. Slowly, we reconnect with the original goodness and strength buried beneath years of alienation from ourselves. Step 4 calls us to accept all of ourselves as worthy. Embracing our wholeness, we move forward as powerful.

Fearless: We do not expect danger as we descend into the depths of our lives. We expect clarity about the nature of our ineffective behaviors. We are unafraid because the "god of our understanding" is no longer a punishing judge. The Steps 4 and 5 are less intimidating as we imagine the non-punitive face of the divine.

Moral: Many of us postpone taking a "moral" inventory for years unable to free ourselves of the lingering images of childhood that shamed and accused us. Karen describes her first response to Step 4: "I have disliked Step 4 as written and interpreted by much of the 12 Step community. It reminds me of the humiliating confessions of my Catholic girlhood."

Freed of the alien energies of shame and guilt, we have become reacquainted with the spontaneity and goodness within us. Our inner spaces have been cleared out and reclaimed as our own. We have become self-possessed. Healed of our deep sense of unworthiness, we no longer look at our ineffective behaviors as evidence of our fundamental sinfulness. This does not excuse us, however, because we accept our responsibility for the consequences of our ineffective behaviors. In Step 4, we embrace the responsibility that is ours.

TAKING A 4ᵗʰ STEP INVENTORY

Step 4 offers us an opportunity to turn mindfulness toward our challenges and concerns. We tend to think of Step 4 as an all-encompassing inventory of our entire pre-recovery lives. More manageably, Step 4 inventories may also be taken around specific issues and relationships. For example:

- A mindful inventory at the end of a relationship.
- A mindful inventory of an old relationship.

- A mindful inventory of your behaviors when attracted to a potential lover.
- A mindful inventory of your relationship with an alcoholic relative or friend.

An inventory acknowledges the two-fold message of life—its trouble and its beauty. Below is a sample inventory taken after a relationship ended. It was taken to bring clarity by uncovering recurring ineffective behaviors and closure by letting go of guilt and resentment. Jennifer made four columns on a piece of paper and labeled them:

1. Ineffective Behaviors: I am finite and limited.
2. Life affirming Behaviors: I am powerful and gifted.
3. Resentments and Disappointments: There were challenges.
4. Gratitude: There was beauty in the relationship.

She then spent time with each column, listing her ineffective behaviors in column 1 and life-affirming behaviors in column 2. Then she listed the resentments and disappointment that had accumulated during the relationship. And finally, the process led Jennifer to list her gratitude for the relationship. After completing each column's reflection, she read the column aloud to herself. At the end of each list, she wrote (and said) these words:

Column 1: I forgive myself.

Column 2: I celebrate myself.

Column 3: I let go.

Column 4: I am grateful.

Column 1: Ineffective Behaviors - I am finite and limited.

1. I ignored my initial concerns about our incompatible definitions of monogamy.

2. I didn't eat regularly. My moodiness confused my lover. I forgive myself.

Column 2: Life-Affirming Behaviors - I am powerful and gifted.

1. I was willing to be his ally and partner in the process of our growth and change.
2. I listened to the inner child and her needs. I celebrate myself.

Column 3: Resentments and Disappointments - There was trouble in the relationship.

1. He never apologized or acknowledged the hurtful consequences of his behavior.
2. Watching TV late at night was his drug of choice at the end of busy days. I let go.

Column 4: Gratitude: There was beauty in the relationship.

Through the pain, I have a deeper understanding of my addiction to betrayal and compulsive people, and a deeper acceptance of my desire for a creative relationship that is not prescribed by the conventional marriage and family script. I am grateful.

MINDFULNESS PRACTICE: STEP 4 SELF-EMPOWERMENT INVENTORY

Choose one (or more) of the following inventories to practice this week:

1. An Inventory of an Old Relationship

A member of Alanon wanted to let go of guilt and resentment and uncover the recurring ineffective behaviors she brought into her intimate relationships.

Column 1: Ineffective Behaviors - I am finite and limited.

- I was too dependent on my last lover. I expected him to love me when I couldn't love myself. He bailed me out when my business was in trouble.
- I didn't express negative emotions. I wasn't able to tell him how much his temper outbursts and need to be in control upset me.
  I forgive myself.

Column 2: Life-affirming Behaviors - I am powerful and gifted.

- I committed myself totally to the relationship. I was faithful.
- I embraced his children and worked hard to be their friend and ally.
  I celebrate myself!

Column 3: Resentments and Disappointments - There was trouble in the relationship.

- He was unwilling to work in therapy on the marriage issue.
- He was bossy when we did projects together. He gave orders.
- He was rigid. He wouldn't share his feelings.
  I let go.

Column 4: Gratitude - There was beauty in the relationship.

- He helped me to take better care of myself by calling doctors sooner.
- He changed my expectation of men for the better.
  I am grateful.

2. An Inventory of Your Behaviors When Attracted to a Potential Lover

A member of Sex and Love Addicts Anonymous took an honest look at her relationship addiction and her ineffective and life-affirming choices.

Column 1: Ineffective Behaviors - I am finite and limited.

- As a result of being attracted to a man in Al-Anon, I tried to control his impression of me by how I dressed and what I shared in meetings.
- I looked through old sign-in pads to see if he had attended previous meetings.
- I attended a meeting for six months where he was a regular even though the meeting was not convenient to my schedule.

  I forgive myself. (or I am becoming willing to forgive myself.)

Column 2: Life affirming - I am powerful and gifted.

- I faced-talked to him instead of running away.
- I eventually made a decision to withdraw from the group where he is a regular.
- I was able to secretary a meeting effectively even when he was in the room.

  I celebrate myself! (or I am becoming willing to celebrate my goodness.)

Column 3 - Resentments: There were challenges.

- He turned away from me after a brief period of moving toward me.
- He immediately got involved with someone else after breaking up with me.

  I let go. (or I am becoming willing to let go.)

Column 4 – Gratitude: There were gifts.

- It's good we didn't initiate a relationship. A break-up would have been painful.
- He triggered my desire to see my mother after many years of no contact.
- Through my obsession with him, I learned about my relationship addiction.

  I am grateful. (or I am willing to become grateful.)

4. An Inventory of Your Relationship with an Alcoholic Relative or Friend

Many women enter Al-Anon caught in the swirls of a drug or alcohol-addicted relative or friend. They are depleted. Their own lives have been set aside as they have devoted all their time and energy in to rescue their friend or child.

Column 1: Ineffective Behaviors - I am finite and limited.

- I put down my son's intellectual gifts.
- I tried to control and manipulate his choice of a mate.
- I let his acting out dominate my life for many years.
- I am easily wounded by things he says and does.
- I trespass his thoughts by overly analyzing his words and actions.
  I forgive myself. (or I am becoming willing to forgive myself.)

Column 2: Life affirming Behaviors - I am powerful and gifted.

- I love him unconditionally. I never gave up on him.
- I gave him structure and a role model for a strong woman.
- I offered him the choice to make something of his life and he took it.
- I made him go to class and finish high school.
  I celebrate myself! (or I am becoming willing to celebrate my goodness.)

Column 3: Resentments - There were challenges.

- He got drunk and acted out at my wedding.
- He is dishonest about his feelings.
- He doesn't confide in me.
- He is clean and sober WITHOUT the program.
- He is oblivious to the wounds inflicted on him by his family of origin.
  I let go. (or I am becoming willing to let go.)

Column 4: Gratitude - There are gifts.

- He is now clean and sober. We have a loving relationship.
- He graduated from high school. He and his mate are going to have a baby.
- He is financially independent.
  I am grateful.

MINDFUL PRACTICE: STEPS 1-4 SELF-EMPOWERMENT INVENTORY

Although the Step 4 stands on its own as a powerful self-empowerment tool, it is most often taken after we have worked the Steps 1-3 around a particular issue or person. Elizabeth, an adult child of an alcoholic parent, used Steps 1-4 to begin her journey into the past to heal into the present. Use her step work to inspire yours.

Steps 1, 2, and 3: My Family of Origin

Step 1: I cannot change the fact that I was born into an alcoholic family. I cannot change the fact that my family never said "I love you" or "You are enough." I feel powerless when present events trigger memories and I feel the pain in my heart more intensely.

Step 2: I have come to believe that a transformational community exists. And that as I share my experience, strength, and hope within that community, I purge the demons that haunt my mind. I hear the words I always longed to hear: "You are loved. You are enough. You are not to blame."

Step 3: I place myself in the stream of power and wisdom flowing in and through my life. I use the tools and strength of the 12 Step community to help me face what comes along. I listen to and learn from the experience, strength, and hope of others. I share my own truth.

A Step 4 Inventory: The Behaviors I Learned in My Family

Column 1: The Ineffective Behaviors I Learned

- I don't communicate my feelings in close relationships.
- I try to take care of other people's needs to the exclusion of my own.
- I didn't learn to express anger. It was safer to be quiet.
- I minimize my problems. It is difficult to ask for help.
- I got good grades so that my parents would love me and pay attention to me.
  I forgive my family. (or I am becoming willing to forgive my family.)

Column 2: The Life-affirming Behaviors I Learned

- I learned financial responsibility at age twelve. I am self-sufficient. I am reliable.
- I value the education my parents provided. I worked hard and got good grades.
- I strive for and meet my goals. I have high standards for myself.
- I am a survivor. I am good in a crisis. I am sensitive to others.
  I celebrate myself! (or I am becoming willing to celebrate my goodness.)

Column 3: The Resentments I Have

- I resent not having had a normal childhood.
- I resent that I was hit by my parents for being an exuberant kid.
- I resent that my parents did not show affection and did not touch us lovingly.
- I resent that I never heard the words, "I love you."
  I let go. (or I am becoming willing to let go.)

Column 4: Gratitude - The Gifts of My Childhood

- I am grateful that my mother served as a role model of a working woman.
- I am grateful that Dad taught me how to dance.
- I am grateful they took us on vacation. They were young and active.
  I am grateful for the gifts of my childhood. (or I am willing to become grateful.)

THE FIFTH STEP—NO MORE SECRETS

Step 5 invites us to celebrate our life-affirming behaviors and accept responsibility for our ineffective behaviors. Most women simply read their Step 4 inventory to a trusted therapist, step group, or sponsor in a relaxed setting. Imagine sharing your 4th step while sitting beside the stream of wisdom or next to your god or goddess. Be inspired by these stories:

I shared my 4th step with my sponsor. I asked her to listen without giving feedback—to witness in respectful silence. After each section, I took a deep breath and with certainty, spoke the ritualized ending.

In a group we listed our positive and negative traits and attitudes. We shared these inventories aloud. I felt the group's support for my honesty and effort. A twenty-pound bag of garbage was lifted from my shoulders. It gave me clarity.

I shared my deepest secrets with my therapist and partner. My trust has grown. I've been released of the sack of guilt and shame I've carried throughout my life. I now share deeply with others and this intimacy invites them to share with me.

I'm "fifth stepping" all the time with my lover. I cannot be intimate unless I'm willing to be vulnerable and honest. As I share the dreaded stuff with him, I experience an exquisite vulnerability, revealing my expanding willingness to love and be loved. I've allowed light to spill on me and my eye is now merciful.

The fifth step also invites you to make a commitment to your own life and transformation. One way to do this is to write a "Vow of Faithfulness" and share it during your fifth step session or during a self-commitment ceremony. Vow composition and ceremony design are explored in more depth in *I Promise Myself* and *A Vow of Faithfulness*.

Amy attended a Vow of Faithfulness Retreat. From early childhood her one all-consuming fantasy was to stand under the "chuppah" (wedding canopy) with her beloved. Tired of this fantasy and the relationship addiction it inspired, she wrote a vow to herself and designed a self-commitment ceremony, which was witnessed by her retreat friends.

Four women held the corners of the chuppah over Amy's head while she recited her vow:

> I, Amy, vow that:
> As I so love the moon, shall I so love myself.
> And as I so love the sound of running creek water,
> Shall I so love myself and the sound of my Inner Voice.
> And as I so love special stones and a certain way sun falls through the leaves,
> Shall I so love what makes me special to myself.
> I will remember that by myself I have everything I need and I am enough.

Turning a merciful eye toward myself, I inventory both my life-affirming and ineffective behaviors, and identify the habits of thought that inspire them.

In the company of trustworthy people, I celebrate my life-affirming behaviors, accept responsibility for my ineffective behaviors, and make a commitment to my transformation.

Chapter 8
In The Fullness of Time

Step 6 and 7 as Written

Were entirely ready to have God remove these defects of character.
Humbly asked God to remove our shortcomings.

Step 6 and 7 as Rewritten

I am entirely ready to deepen my inner well-being by relinquishing my negative habits of behavior and cultivating new thoughts to inspire healthier behaviors and outcomes.

My life journey is orchestrated by my own inner wisdom.
In the fullness of time, I am transformed at a deeper level of my being. I actively participate in this process.

REFRAMING DEFECT LANGUAGE

Imagine that it didn't happen the way you were told in the religious communities of childhood. Imagine hearing Eve's words read from the sacred text one morning at your church, synagogue, mosque, or women's circle:

> As the Mother of all Living, I pick the fruit of life. It is good and satisfies hunger. It is pleasant to the eye. It is wise and opens the way to self-discovery and understanding. Those among you who are curious, who lust for life in all its fluidity, dare with me—bite into your life and the fullness of its possibility.

After Eve's words are read, the elder women give an apple to the first person in the row. As the crone hands you an apple, she looks into your eyes and says:

> Take and eat of the good fruit of life. You are good. You are very good. Bite into the apple and savor its sweetness.

80

After everyone has partaken of the good fruit of life, the closing blessing is spoken:

> *Open to the depths of goodness within you. Believe in your goodness. Live out of the abundance of who you are as a child of life. Affirm the original goodness of your children until the stories of old hold no sway in their hearts. Bite into your life and the fullness of its possibility.*

As we dismantle the throne of god, traditional religion's hierarchically-based answers to the fundamental questions of human existence must be reformulated from our own experience. As the image of the big guy in the heavens, scrutinizing our every thought and action dissolves, and as his system of rewards and punishments, keeping us in line, is disbanded, women are reframing traditional religion's definitions of sin, salvation, and surrender and recovery's definitions of defects of character.

Ascent has been the journey of men. They erect ladders and monuments, reaching toward the heavens. They name their gods "Higher Power" and "God of the High Places." They have accurately defined their sin as pride and the desire to be god. In a society that worships a male god and prefers men, these have not been our sins.

God-likeness has never been an option for us. Our place has been clearly secondary and supportive. The root of our sin has been an alienation from ourselves and an accompanying self-critical spirit. We have internalized the systems of thought and belief that take for granted our defectiveness.

We sin by our own participation in a hierarchical paradigm that at its foundation is not woman or life-affirming and by our cooperation in the maintenance of this paradigm in the training of our daughters and granddaughters. We sin each time we ask "what's wrong with me;" each time we waste a precious resource of time, money, or energy in our frantic search for remedies; each time we twist ourselves out of shape in response to an "expert" opinion.

We sin as we hide our bodies beneath layers of clothing, our natural processes beneath layers of secrecy, our sexuality beneath layers of passivity, our opinions and thoughts beneath layers of conformity, and our feelings beneath layers of restraint.
We sin as we hide the reality of our lives beneath layers of seething resentment in response to and in avoidance of the persistent scrutiny of the culture, of god, and eventually, of ourselves.

As we redefine sin, we rethink the remedies put forward to alleviate our sinful condition as well. Men's sins have been pride and grandiosity so it makes sense that ego-deflation, denial of self, and "surrender to god's will" have been the accepted remedies. Our alienation from self and all-consuming self-critical attitude require a conversion of sorts. We turn inward — instead of looking to a god or higher power outside of our lives for salvation, we journey "home" to ourselves.

Instead of ascending to enlightened states that involve the denial of self, we have discovered that ours is a journey of descent—we look deep within to reclaim forgotten aspects of ourselves. We reach beneath our obsession with flaws, beneath the accomplishments that mask our sense of unworthiness, beneath years of alienation from ourselves, toward the goodness at our center. We discover that the good is deeply embedded within us. As we embrace our original goodness, our inner spaces are cleared out and reclaimed as our own. We find rest within our own lives and accept all of ourselves as worthy.

No longer scrutinizing every facet of our beings to figure out what is wrong, we celebrate ourselves as powerful and gifted children of life. Refusing to speak of defects of character, we affirm: "I am good not bad. I am not defective. I was taught ineffective behaviors that do not support my recovery. As I heal into the present, I reconnect to my original goodness. From it, my life-affirming behaviors flow."

IN THE FULLNESS OF TIME

At a chaplaincy training seminar, we were told the story of a camper, who noticed a moth pushing, straining, and struggling to get out of its cocoon. It was a disturbing sight to the camper, and when she could take it no longer, she extended the tiny slit-opening of the cocoon. The moth was freed and fell to the ground and died. The camper was devastated. Her intention had been to help.

Inspired by the story, I investigated the moth's life. Its life-cycle from egg to adult moth is orchestrated by a remarkable inner mechanism of "right timing" that leads to each new transformation. This timing allows for the larva's emergence to coincide with an adequate food supply, for the outgrowing of its skins, and for the location of the cocoon until the conditions are ready for its survival as an adult moth.

Even the moth's struggle against the walls of the cocoon supports its metamorphosis by strengthening its wings and releasing fluids to enhance its coloring. The camper, unaware of the trustworthiness of timing and the sacredness of struggle in the moth's cycle, cut open the cocoon. This premature release led to the death of the moth. Swirling in her own discomfort, she had arrogantly intruded in the moth's life process. Yet the moth was content in the midst of its own trustworthy process, a process essential to its development.

Like the moth, you are an emerging healthy adult whose process is orchestrated by a finely tuned inner timing. In the fullness of time, when a behavior begins to hamper, press, and squeeze, you twist and turn until you burst out of the old skin and are freed at a deeper level of your existence. Each time a memory or feeling is ready to be acknowledged out of decades of denial, it gnaws its way to the surface through a dream or sensory memory, through a movie, or by reading / hearing the stories of others. In the fullness of time, it is remembered or felt. The trustworthy timing of your Inner Wisdom leads to each new transformation when you are ready. Attending your first support group, women's circle, or 12 Step meeting was an indication of being "entirely ready."

STEPS 6 AND 7 MINDFULNESS PRACTICE

Our recovery journey is orchestrated by Deeper Wisdom. In the fullness of time, we become entirely ready to have our injuries healed and ineffective behaviors transformed. One way to actively participate in this transformational process is by practicing the Step 6 and 7's Mindfulness Practice, which includes the four reflections outlined below.

1. Identify Your Ineffective Behaviors to Determine Readiness. List four of your ineffective behaviors. Rank them according to "readiness." As you list them, you will know which ones you are ready to work on. For example:

- I do not take care of myself: I do not go to the doctor. I do not eat regularly.
- I ignore aches and pains. I live as if I am going to die at 50.
- I do not trust myself in relationships.
- I ignore danger signals in relationships and live in potentiality, not reality. I am easily seduced by charming males.

2. Identify the Underlying Formative Experiences

Focusing solely on behaviors will not reach deep enough to bring about sustainable transformation. We must uncover the formative events that shaped our thoughts. These thoughts hold our behaviors in place. What formative event shaped the #1 ineffective behavior you listed in the exercise above? For example:

> "I was neglected as a child. It was not safe to tell anyone that my body hurt, my head ached, or that I was hungry. I was told I would die if I told the truth. I now tell the truth in my life. There is an old belief that this is dangerous and will lead to death."

3. The Readiness Statement

Write a statement of your readiness. Within your statement, list the healing resources and tools of support available to support your readiness. For example:

> "I am ready to take care of my body and life with tenderness and care. I am ready to see a doctor once a year to honor my body and health."

4. The Request

Write a request (prayer) to your Deeper Wisdom, Intuition, Community of Support, or whatever image you embraced in Step 2 as your "higher power." For example:

> "Dear Deeper Wisdom, as I turn toward the resources available to me, I trust the faithful process of healing and transformation to unfold. I ask that I might, one day at a time, learn to take care of my body with care and constancy."

Women's Stories

Allow the following examples of the Step 6-7 Process to inspire and inform your practice. Three ineffective behaviors are highlighted: perfectionism, care-taking, and judgmentalism.

1. Perfectionism

Ineffective Behavior: I have outrageously unrealistic expectations of myself. I must produce perfect articles that inspire the admiration of my colleagues. In relationships, I must be the other person's best-loved friend. In my inner life, I must have a perfect recovery, boundless energy, and unending creativity.

Formative Experience: My family desperately needed to look good on the outside because it was so sick inside. I was not allowed to make mistakes. I was criticized no matter how well I did at school or home. I could never be, do, or have enough.

Readiness: I am ready to let go of perfectionism. I will make a conscious effort not to be the best at work. Every time I have the urge to become #1, I will stop and reflect on the origins of this compulsion. I shift to new thoughts: "I no longer need to be the best to have a place and voice on this earth." I will ask a friend to listen to me.

Request/Prayer: Deeper Wisdom, give me faith that I will be loved even if I am not perfect. Promise me that if I live a normal, human life, I will not disappear to the people important to me. Help me find compassion for my failings and limitations. Do not let me pass on the curse of perfectionism to my children. Let us sincerely believe we are enough, even wonderful, just as we are.

2. Caretaking by Giving Advice

Ineffective Behavior: I give advice to others.

Formative Experience: It's hard for me to simply witness another person's problem or pain. I must do something about their problem or try to take away their pain. I was raised with people who gave unsolicited advice and who were not capable of simply being witnesses. I didn't learn how to help another except by giving advice. I still use advice-giving to avoid the feelings that come up when I truly listen.

Readiness: I am ready to stop giving advice. I am ready to listen to others, knowing I cannot fix their problem or take away their pain without feeling out of integrity with myself. I am willing to learn how to be a caring witness and accept the uncomfortable feelings that come up.

Request/Prayer: Breath and the Wise Center you bring me into contact with, I ask that you stay with me as I endeavor to be an open and caring witness of my friends and family's lives without giving advice unless it is asked for.

3. Judgmental of Others

Ineffective Behavior: I'm judgmental.

Formative Experience: I learned to be judgmental from my parents. I judged others as a way to hold myself above them and boost my fragile self-esteem.

Readiness: I am ready to stop judging others as morally, intellectually, and emotionally inferior to me. I have strong self-esteem, which does not need to be propped up by denigrating others. I can learn from and love others when I withhold my judgments of them. This I am ready to do.

Request/Prayer: Breath, be my companion as I endeavor to suspend judgment. Support me to hold myself in high esteem and enable me to accept others on their own terms.

MINDFULNESS PRACTICE: STEPS 1, 2, 3, 6, AND 7

Although the Sixth and Seventh Steps are most often taken after we have worked Step 4, there is no one right way to move through the Steps. As we become familiar with them and practice them in all our affairs, we weave them into our ongoing life journey to experience clarity and transformation. Be inspired by Josie's use of the Steps 1, 2, 3, 6, and 7 as her own rituals of self-empowerment and transformation.

Mindfulness Practice: Josie's Steps

As a member of Al-Anon, detached from the swirls of her alcoholic son, she was confronted with her own ineffective behaviors. Initially she took the first three Steps concerning her son, she now personalized them to deal with her relationship to food and deepened her reflection in Steps 6 and 7.

Steps 1, 2, and 3

Step 1: I am powerless over my misuse of food for a multitude of purposes other than nutritional sustenance. Sometimes my life is unmanageable as a result and sometimes it seems altogether manageable. But always in the background a voice says I should be able to control these eating impulses. I am powerless over that voice. I am powerless over the fact that disassociate from my body and use food to substitute for feeling. Perhaps the admission of my powerlessness over my misuse of food will free me in many of the ways taking the first step around my son's alcoholism did.

Step 2: I believe a healing community exists which can help me change my ineffective behaviors. I have come to believe that there's an appropriate time in my life for each area to be worked on. I have given up the notions that I must work on them all at once and that if I'm not working on my distorted body image all the time I can't be happy or well. I have come to believe in progress not perfection.

Step 3: I choose to trust in my own unique timetable for addressing my food disorders and body disassociation. I make a decision to spend one hour a week reflecting on this issue and focusing on how to work the Steps around it. During this hour I will listen to my Inner Voice. I choose to pay attention to this Voice and to follow where it leads me.

Steps 6 and 7

Ineffective Behavior: I use food inappropriately to dull my feelings and escape pain. I am inactive. I get depressed. I isolate and don't reach out for the resources I have. I only reach out when I'm feeling positive because something feels deeply wrong about expressing my sadness, fears, and feelings. I use food, TV, and depression to keep from acknowledging those parts of myself that I feel are inappropriate.

Formative Experiences: As a child, I was expected to be wonderful. My parents were busy people who had no time for me and no tolerance for me to be imperfect. I got it at an early age that I was only acceptable when I was sweet, happy, singing, and perfect. As a growing girl full of inappropriate and imperfect thoughts and feelings, I retreated to my room so that I wouldn't infect my parents with my imperfection. My parents were more than willing to have me stay in my room and only emerge when I was "civilized."

Readiness: I'm ready to share my shameful thoughts and feelings with my support community, program friends, sponsor, and therapist. I'm willing to be aware when these escape tendencies overwhelm me and I will make an effort to use the resources of music, nature, and spiritual community to heal myself of the shame.

Request/Prayer: Sacred Spirit, fill me with courage to face into the dark places. Help me to break my isolation and reach out for support. Help me to acknowledge my thoughts and feelings rather than using covering-up tactics. Help me to celebrate all the frightened parts of me, which are as sacred as the wise, witty, and charming parts. I am entirely ready to deepen my inner well-being by relinquishing my negative habits of behavior and cultivating new thoughts to inspire healthier behaviors and outcomes.

My life journey is orchestrated by my own inner wisdom.
In the fullness of time, I am transformed at a deeper level
of my being. I actively participate in this process.

Chapter 9
Taking Responsibility

Step 8 and 9 as Written

Made a list of all persons we had harmed and became willing to make amends to them all.

Made direct amends to such people wherever possible, except when to do so would injure them or others.

Step 8 and 9 as Rewritten

Certain that I love myself, I welcome clarity in my relationships. I acknowledge those who were hurt and those who were enriched by my habits of behaviors.

Having forgiven myself, I take active responsibility by making amends to those I harmed, except when to do so would further injure them or others.

In Step 4, we acknowledged both our life-affirming behaviors and our ineffective behaviors. As we continue our journey out of denial, Step 8 and 9 encourage us to turn our awareness toward the consequences of these behaviors in the lives of others. Certain that we love ourselves, we risk and welcome clarity and honesty in our relationships. There are several possible ways to make amends.

1. As we come out of denial, our current transformation is an amend to ourselves and others for the ineffective behaviors of our past.

> "I have changed many aspects of my life. I seek healthy relationships and compassionate people. I have stopped overworking and over-drinking. I have started to speak honestly. I have learned how to set limits, ask for help, and

exercise my voice. My current life is an amend for my former life."

2. A direct amend may involve an acknowledgment to the person or persons who bore the brunt of our ineffective behaviors.

> "During my college years I acted out of my own self-rejection in jealousy toward women. One friend bore the brunt of this ineffective behavior. I was jealous of her beauty. In insidious ways I kept her from interacting with my friends. I was afraid she would take their love and attention away from me.
>
> Her presence seemed life-threatening at times. Years later as I understood the effect of my formative experiences, I remembered her. She had been a supportive friend through high school and college and then, as a result of the strain of my jealousy, we had drifted apart. I made direct amends to her in a letter, acknowledging my jealousy and the ways I had acted out toward her. I thanked her for her support and wished her well in her current endeavors."

3. An amend may involve compensation for injury or loss.

Through a fourth step, an Al-Anon member became aware of the ways she'd neglected her children as a result of addictive relationships with men. She used the family's limited resources of food and money to bail out the men who came and went from their lives. At times she didn't have lunch money for her children. As she worked the Steps and slowly disengaged from the swirls of men, she chose to compensate her children by making a firm commitment to three life-affirming behaviors:

- She arranged a non-negotiable weekly food shopping trip as a family outing.
- She prepared daily lunches in gratitude for the children's presence in her life.

- She started a savings account for each child as a tribute to their future dreams.

PRACTICING STEPS 8 AND 9: RIVALS

Competition among women is woven into the fabric of a society that prefers men. We compete with each other for the attention of men. Inundated with cultural and religious attitudes fostering rivalry and suspicion among women, we lose touch with our original connection to the women in our lives. They function merely as fill-in companions between lovers. Inundated with homophobic messages, we become even more deeply alienated from each other and the organic resources available in women-centered relationships. Like the steady drip of an IV inserted at birth, we absorb attitudes and fears designed to keep us separate. Add your stories to theirs:

> "I was groomed to compete with women. I feel tremendous jealousy. I don't know how to release it. At the very core of it, I am afraid that our closeness will violate the tenet that I have to compete. And I fear that if I get too close to women, I will be attracted to them and then my lesbian phobia comes up."

> "I was taught that men only want one thing—namely sex with a beautiful woman and that a woman had to be cooperative to keep a man. This left me out and I've been jealous of attractive, outgoing women all my life. I tend to judge attractive women as superficial and assume they look down on those of us not as beautiful. These judgments and assumptions have kept me from being open to women and from experiencing healing through our common experiences."

> "My most comfortable relationships today are with women. Yet I painfully acknowledge that for most of my life, I had to feel more attractive than a woman to include

her in my life. She must pose no threat and there must be no possibility of competition between us. I instantly sized up women, and when I felt out of their league, I became intimidated and jealous. I expressed these feelings indirectly through gossip and a critical attitude."

At some point during our work together I encourage women to inventory their attitudes, relationships, and behaviors toward other women. Steps 8 and 9 offer us an opportunity to confront these behaviors and move beyond them. A participant in ADW recovery circle took the challenge and looked at her personal and professional relationships with women. Steps 8 and 9 guided her through this reflection.

Step 8: List those you have hurt through jealousy, gossip, triangular affairs, passive aggressive anger, and diminishing the reputation of another.

> "I was jealous of my friend's wife while visiting their home. She is a very organized cook and hostess. I felt smothered by it all and wanted to spend time with my friend, rather than with her. I expressed my jealousy indirectly through criticism and smoldering anger."

Step 9: Determine if making direct amends (acknowledgment to the person) is appropriate.

If yes, write a statement of your intention to carry out the amends in specific terms.

> "When we are together again I'll make amends to myself by acknowledging my need to spend more time with my friend. He's been in my life for many years and time with him is important to me. I'll acknowledge my feelings of inadequacy in the face of her competence. I will also make a practice of expressing appreciation for her talents."

If no, how will you make amends through your changed behavior in the present?

> "My colleagues and I struggle to keep from feeling inferior so we compete with each other for men's attention. I will make amends by giving women support, rather than striving to receive the approval of men. I will affirm our solidarity."

MINDFULNESS PRACTICE: STEPS 6, 7, 8, and 9

Although the 8th and 9th Steps stand on their own as a powerful self-empowerment tool, most often they are taken after we have worked Steps 6 and 7.

> *Example 1: Andrea, an Al-Anon member used Steps 6 and 7 to list and rank her ineffective behaviors. She determined that she was ready to change her habit of indirect communication. Her "readiness" list:*

> Steps 6 and 7: My List to Determine Readiness

> 1. Indirect communication - Entirely Ready!
> 2. Bodily neglect - Ready.
> 3. Isolation - Working on readiness.
> 4. Repressed anger and sadness - Not Ready.

Andrea continued the Step 6 and 7 process to discover the nature of this ineffective behavior and commit to transformation. She then used Step 8 and 9 to list those harmed by her indirect communication and to determine if direct or indirect amends were warranted.

Step 6: Uncovering the Nature of this Ineffective Behavior

Ineffective Behavior: Indirect communication with people. When I think or feel something, I keep silent or drop hints, hoping people will get what I mean. I deal with my anger or outrage when something doesn't feel right by nagging my loved ones with accusation and blame.

Formative Experiences: I learned to communicate indirectly from my family of origin. As a child, I was not encouraged to say "No" if something did not feel right to me. I was not encouraged to discover how I really felt or thought. I was told how I ought to feel and think. To stray from the "should" was terrifying. As a child I was not safe stating my needs or wants. I survived by meeting the needs of others.

Step 7: Acknowledging my Readiness to Transform this Behavior

Readiness: I am ready to express who I am and what I need, feel, and think. I trust that I am held by my support community and my sense of worth and confidence. I trust that as I learn to express myself I will not be abandoned or shamed. I trust the ADW process to assist me to transform my indirectness into more direct, honest ways of relating.

Step 8: Those Splattered by Indirect Communication

Harm: My husband and children bear the brunt of my indirectness and repressed emotions. My language is full of self-righteous blame, which leaves scars. When I become overwhelmed by my responsibilities and commitments, I ignore my well-being while attending to the family, which leads to episodes of irrational ranting and raving. This is the indirect way I act out my repressed anger.

Step 9: Direct or Indirect Amends

Direct Amends: I've acknowledged to my husband the inappropriateness of my habit of nagging. I have also acknowledged my inappropriate intrusions into my daughter's life.

Indirect Amends: I have made the most substantial amends by making changes for the better within myself. I'm more present with my emotions. I'm learning to be more assertive about my needs. I have taken the blaming talk out of my language and I'm learning to communicate with my loved ones with greater clarity and honesty.

> *Example 2: Josie, a member of Debtors Anonymous, offers us another example of using a sequence of Steps to move from "readiness" to action. She looked at her relationship to money using Steps 6 and 7. She then listed those who bore the brunt of her ineffective behaviors in Step 8, and determined if direct or indirect amends were called for in Step 9.*

Step 6: Uncovering the Nature of this Ineffective Behavior

Ineffective Behaviors: I do not utilize my resources well. I spend compulsively for instant gratification at restaurants and movies. My essential needs go unmet. I end up with no prudent reserve to buy contact lenses and work shoes. I am unable to carry out my financial responsibilities to my daughter. Deprivation and instant gratification go hand in hand—I deprive myself of the experiences I need to round out my life.

Formative Experiences: In my family of origin, there was never enough love, money, or attention so my attitude became "it won't be there later, so use it now." My mom was addicted to her husband—we couldn't buy the things I needed because only my step-father was free to use the money. His snack food and pornography stashes were well-stocked. I grew up feeling cheated. I was determined to never again feel deprived. I ended up deprived anyway because I didn't develop a self-caring discipline around the use of money.

Step 7: Acknowledging my Readiness to Transform this Behavior

Readiness: I am ready to stop acting out of a pattern of deprivation. I can take care of myself by looking further ahead than the moment at hand. I will utilize the tools of support made available to me in Debtor's Anonymous. I will continue to attend meetings, meet with my budget support group, make program calls before I spend compulsively, and one day at a time face into my financial obligations.

Step 8: Those Splattered by my Ineffective Financial Behaviors Harm: My daughter lives with her dad and my patterns affect them long distance. They bear the brunt of my behaviors. I don't consistently pay child support, which limits her standard of living. Folks from whom I borrowed and never repaid have been affected by my behaviors. The pain of these consequences keeps me committed to recovery.

Step 9: Direct or Indirect Amends

Amends: I have thanked my ex-husband for his patience and understanding. I'm taking steps to rectify the child support situation. I'm making amends to all of us by being in Debtors Anonymous and working my program which means:

- Being willing to abstain from compulsive spending and debting.
- Developing a spending plan in order to move out of financial vagueness.
- Keeping records of all my spending in a clear and concise manner.
- Working towards solvency and living in abundance.
- Moving out of under-earning and underachieving.

Certain that I love myself, I welcome clarity in my relationships. I acknowledge those who were hurt by my ineffective habits of behaviors. Having forgiven myself, I take active responsibility by making amends to those I harmed except when to do so would further injure them or others.

Chapter 10
The Gift and Challenge of Life

Step 10 as Written

Continued to take personal inventory and when we were wrong promptly admitted it.

Step 10 as Rewritten

Choosing to be present in my own life, I acknowledge the gifts and challenges of the day, celebrate my life-affirming behaviors, and take responsibility for my ineffective ones.

In the very beginning, the girl-child is interested in herself and involved in self-motivated adventures. She moves through each day with an exuberant strength, a remarkable energy, and a contagious liveliness. Every experience is filled with wonder and awe. It is enough to gaze at the redness of an apple and watch the water flow over the rocks in a stream. She is a natural explorer of everything in her world. Life is her teacher, challenge, and delight. She is never bored. There is always another adventure and project to turn toward. Her ordinary life is interesting enough.

As she moves through childhood, this vitality dies. From her first reading of *Sleeping Beauty*, she longs to be delivered from ordinary life and transported to the realm of fairy tales. She turns away from the Vital One she once was. Her intimate connection to life's unfolding is severed. No longer is ordinary life her challenge, inspiration, and delight; it is boring. She waits for a savior to come along and rescue her from "ordinary life."

She longs for human saviors: "if only" she had a different partner, job, or family; a life-changing insight or treatment; a big lottery win. She longs for divine saviors: "if only" a vision from heaven, a miracle, a definite word from god/goddess/higher power through her therapist or guru. Her life remains on hold as she waits for the deliverer to come. Eventually, she needs a drug of some sort—alcohol, a lover, an adrenaline rush—to feel what she once felt spontaneously in the midst of her ordinary life.

Step 10 reminds us of what we once knew: "Vital One, you move through life with an exuberant strength, remarkable energy, and contagious liveliness. Your ordinary life is interesting enough. It will be your teacher, healer, challenge, inspiration, and delight. Embrace it with respect. Express it with all the colors of the rainbow. Trust its lessons above the prescriptions of experts. Your ordinary life is good. It is very good."

A DAILY STEP 10 MINDFULNESS PRACTICE

A daily inventory invites us to reflect upon the two-fold nature of life: its blessing and its challenge. A daily inventory invites us to take responsibility for our two-fold response to life: life-affirming behaviors based on gratitude and ineffective behaviors based on resentment.

Taking a daily inventory lightens our load as we travel through life. We take care of business each day. Thus, the moment is no longer cluttered with accumulated resentment, guilt, and unfinished business. Taking a daily inventory reminds us that our lives, our precious ordinary lives, are our teachers, healers, and challenge. Daily life is the curriculum life offers us. All we need to heal, learn, and grow is made manifest within our own lives.

Look back on your day: Acknowledge both life's blessing and its challenge, and take responsibility for your response to life. Just as you did to prepare for the 4th Step, make four columns on a large piece of paper.

Label the columns:

1. Ineffective Behaviors: I am finite and limited.
2. Life affirming Behaviors: I am powerful and gifted.
3. Resentments and Disappointments: There were challenges today.
4. Gratitude: There were gifts today.

After completing your daily inventory, read each column aloud to yourself. At the end of each list write (and say) these words:

Column 1: I forgive myself. (Or, I am becoming willing to forgive myself.)
Column 2: I celebrate myself! (Or, I am becoming willing to celebrate my goodness.)
Column 3: I let go. (Or, I am becoming willing to let go.)
Column 4: I am grateful. (Or, I am willing to become grateful.)

Turn toward your daily life with renewed attention. Infuse it with consciousness. Live it with clarity, joy, and gratitude. Here are some Step 10 inventories to inspire you.

Jessica's Tenth Step

Ineffective Behaviors: I am finite and limited.
    I didn't eat regularly today. My moodiness was erratic and confused my children. I forgive myself. I choose to take better care of myself tomorrow.

Life-Affirming Behaviors: I am powerful and gifted.
    Today I was reminded of my goodness: I responded to music, my son's smile, and my husband's touch. I truly heard my friend's voice and felt heard by her. I looked at the sky and sighed a deep sigh. I cleaned my house. I kept my center. I celebrate my willingness to live in the moment.

Resentments and Disappointments: There was challenge today. My husband seldom apologizes for his ineffective behaviors. As I let go of resentment I discover life-affirming strategies for my challenges.

Gratitude: There was blessing today. I walked with a friend. We share the stuff that really matters. This was a gift. I am grateful for the blessing of my friend today.

Julia's Tenth Step

Ineffective Behaviors: I am finite and limited. Today it was difficult to accept constructive criticism from my boss.I forgive myself. My boss is my teacher and I will extract every lesson life has to teach me through him. When I have nothing more to learn, I'll move on.

Life-Affirming Behaviors: I am powerful and gifted. Today a man expressed appreciation for something I said that gave him an insight into his relationship with his daughter who is my age.I celebrate my willingness to share my life experiences with people.

Resentments and Disappointments: There was challenge today. I'm disappointed I didn't get an A+ review from my boss.As I let go, I discover creative strategies for my job challenges.

Gratitude: There were gifts today. Today was my weekly massage date. This is the best treat I give to myself.I am grateful for the blessing of my life today.

Sharon's Tenth Step

Ineffective Behaviors: I am finite and limited. I gave my sister unsolicited advice instead of listening to her non-judgmentally. *I forgive myself. My sister reminds me that her life is her own to lead. She will ask for support when she wants it.*

Life-Affirming Behaviors: I am powerful and gifted.
Today I became aware of my effectiveness as I noticed the way my students respond when I encourage their originality by minimizing structure and control.
I celebrate my capacity to teach and my willingness to allow creative chaos.

Resentments and Disappointments: There were challenges today.
My landlord is constantly changing our agreements to suit his whims. I resent being at his mercy as a renter.
As I let go, I discover creative strategies for my housing challenges.

Gratitude: There were gifts today.
My friends gave me love and support today.
I am grateful for the blessing of my friends today.

Kathleen's Tenth Step

Ineffective Behaviors: I am finite and limited.
I am unable to ask for what I need. My office is a mezzanine space that get too hot. Rather than ask for AC to be turned down, I changed into my dress.
I forgive myself. My job reminds me to ask for what I want and need as I observe others taking care of themselves effortlessly.

Life-Affirming Behaviors: I am powerful and gifted.
Today I received a program call from someone who'd just been laid off from his job. I was able to listen without giving advice or making judgments.
I celebrate my compassion and capacity to listen to and support my friends.

Resentments and Disappointments: There were challenges today.
Today I received a call from a friend who talks non-stop. I resent that I am the one who must learn to set firm boundaries.
As I let go of my resentment, I take responsibility to set my own limits with behaviors that do not work for me.

Gratitude: There were gifts today.

During lunch I enjoyed a walk on the pier. I could appreciate the sky, water, birds, and beautiful skyline. Simple things delight me.

I'm grateful for simple things of beauty.

GRATITUDE: THE ESSENTIAL MINDFULNESS PRACTICE

I first learned about gratitude as a potential response to life when my recovering alcoholic husband announced that he was having an affair and wanted a divorce. I ran to my Al-Anon sponsor for help to manage my swirling anxious thoughts. She challenged me to resist the impulse to fall into the enormous chasm of fear triggered by the thought of a divorce in 18 months.

Ginny encouraged me to stay present during every moment of the experience and to maintain a daily gratitude practice of acknowledging the goodness of life even as the world around and within me was falling apart. She promised me that if I stayed present, that I would be ready for that far-off day when the "no-fault" divorce would be finalized.

By the time he and I met at the courthouse 18 months later, I was studying at Princeton Theological Seminary and in love with my new life of study, exploration, and writing. As we embraced after the divorce proceedings, I offered him the blessing of gratitude, "I'm grateful for the gift you gave me. Yes, my world crashed when you left, but it needed to crash. The life I live today is more authentic and joyful. Peace be with you."

I have continued that almost-daily gratitude practice for over 3 decades and have explored the important role gratitude plays in our happiness, healthy adjustment to life's twists and turns, and physical well-being. I have come to believe that gratitude, as a response to life, is a cost-effective way to manage our anxiety and to increase our body, mind, and spirit wellness.

Gratitude and Well-Being

Gratitude is one of the most effective interventions to shift the content of our thoughts. This is because the positive emotion of gratitude changes our brain chemistry. The brain is a single processor, which means it can only process one thing at a time. When you focus on the things you appreciate in your life, there's no space in the brain for anger, complaint, or worry. In this way, gratitude contributes to our well-being.

According to Dr. Robert Emmons and Dr. Michael McCullough, who edited the first scholarly volume devoted to a fundamental human quality of gratitude, there are many emotions and personality traits important to well-being, but gratitude is uniquely important. They focused on gratitude as an emotion. In their scientific experiments, individuals were asked to keep track of their experiences of gratitude.

Emmons and McCullough found that when individuals kept track of their gratitude, they experienced more gratitude and more of the positive changes associated with it.

Grateful people experience these qualities of well-being:

1. Grateful people are happier and more satisfied with their lives and relationships.
2. They have higher levels of self-acceptance and greater authority and control of their circumstances, their personal growth, and the purposeful use of their capacities.
3. They have more positive ways of coping with life's difficulties because they are more likely to seek support from others and grow from the experience.
4. They have fewer negative coping strategies because they are less likely to avoid or deny the problem, blame others for it, or cope through substance use.

5. They have fewer experiences of bitterness, resentment, irritation, and envy. They may experience these negative reactions initially, but grateful people tend to pivot/shift toward gratitude as their primary response.

6. They cope better during life transitions because they are more grateful before the transition, they are less stressed and depressed during the transition, and more satisfied with their lives after the transition.

7. They sleep better because their responses are less reactive and more peaceful. The practice of shifting our thoughts from complaint to gratitude strengthens our neural pathways to look for what's good in our lives, which then makes it easier for our brains to find things to appreciate. Strengthen your gratitude "muscle" by using it. Incorporate this chapter's Step 10 practices and gratitude meditations into your daily routine.

Step Ten Reflection: Self-Awareness Journal (SAJ)

In your SAJ respond to each of these classic gratitude quotes. How do they inspire, challenge, and enrich your understanding and practice of gratitude?

"Gratitude is so close to the bone of life, pure and true, that it instantly stops the rational mind, and all its planning and plotting. That kind of let go is fiercely threatening. I mean, where might such gratitude end?" -Regina Sara Ryan

"Life is swift and precious while it's in our grasp. Loving yourself is such a small act of appreciation for the everlasting Love that has breathed you into being and on whose wings you will be carried when it's time to leave this life." -Paula M. Reeves

"Focusing on this very moment is a powerful practice. Being grateful for what's happening now can be uplifting even if the moment before we felt down. A feedback loop can then

emerge where the more thankful we become, the more connected we feel to ourselves, one another, and the planet."
-Susan Greenland

"Gratitude unlocks the fullness of life. It turns what we have into enough, and more. It turns problems into gifts, failures into success, the unexpected into perfect timing, and mistakes into important events. Gratitude makes sense of our past, brings peace for today, and creates a vision for tomorrow."
-Melodie Beattie

"Embrace your ordinary life, whatever its wrapping, for in the embrace you will hear the whisper of Gratitude. Listen for her in the ordinary activities of your day, the ordinary encounters with loved ones, and the ordinary challenges that greet you each morning. She speaks from the depths of you, in the voice of your ordinary life." -Patricia Lynn Reilly

Choosing to be present in my own life, I acknowledge the gifts and challenges of the day with gratitude, celebrate my life-affirming behaviors, and take responsibility for my ineffective ones.

Chapter 11
Making Conscious Contact

Step 11 as Written

Sought through prayer and meditation to improve our conscious contact with God as we understood him, praying only for knowledge of his will for us and the power to carry that out.

Step 11 as Rewritten

Through mindful reflection, I place myself in stream of wisdom flowing through my life. I make conscious contact with my truest self and clearest thought.

While at a mindfulness retreat, I was reminded of a Harry Chapin story-song about a vibrant child who picked up crayons excitedly on the first day of school. She filled the paper with flowers of every color. Her drawing disturbed the teacher and she asked the child what she was doing. "I'm painting flowers," the child answered.

The teacher reprimanded her: "Flowers are red and leaves are green. There's no need to see colors any other way than the way they've always been seen." The child exclaimed: "Oh, no! There are so many colors in the rainbow... so many colors in the morning sun... so many colors in the flowers... And I see every one."

The teacher called the child sassy and placed her in the corner with these words, "There's a way things should be done. You must draw flowers in the same colors and shapes they've always been drawn." At a time when the child needed encouragement of her originality and creativity, she was shamed and ostracized. She was convinced by her isolation that it's wrong to follow her own creative instincts.

Frightened and lonely, she recanted, parroting the teacher's words: "Flowers are red and leaves are green. There's no need to see flowers any other way than the way they've always been seen." Years later the child moved to another school. Her new teacher said that drawing should be fun, "There are so many colors in the rainbow, so many colors in the morning sun, so many colors in the flowers. You can use every one!" Unmoved, the child painted flowers in neat rows of green and red.

Harry Chapin's story illustrates the evolution of our spirituality. In the very beginning of our lives we have direct access to the spirit of life. It is as near to us as the breath that fills us. And it connects us to everything. We are not alone. Our spirit is one with the spirit of our beloved grandmother, of our favorite rock, tree, and star. We develop our own special methods for contacting the spirit in all things.

Our imaginations are free for a time. We do not need priests or teachers to describe the divine to us. Spirit erupts spontaneously in colorful and unique expressions. God is grandma, the twinkling evening star, the gentle breeze that washes across our face, the peaceful quiet darkness after everyone has fallen asleep, and all the colors of the rainbow.

Eventually, we find our way into the open spaces of spirituality. We learn again what we knew as children, to use all the colors of the rainbow in the expression of our spirituality. Add to the following list the creative ways you pray, reflect, and meditate, ways that move beyond the prescriptions of family and religion.

> Dance a prayer inspired by your favorite music. Dance, allowing the life-force to move through you in merriment.

> Walk in the forest as a walking meditation, honoring the beauty of all creation.

Walk in a protest march, each step a peace-prayer in honor of the Earth.

Write in your journal and listen to your personal truth. Write a daily gratitude list, affirming the abundance and grace of your life.

Enjoy a massage as a tender prayer for your body. Enjoy a long, hot bath with candles and oil as a body-loving meditation.

"Swimming is my meditation. I feel held, contained, nurtured, and at one with the water. I lose awareness of everything except the water, my body and breath."

"I take time out from the busyness of the day and make a cup of tea. Then I sit down and put all my attention onto that cup of tea: its smell, taste, temperature and appearance. This meditation is refreshing, and doesn't require much time."

"I take a special view of the time spent waiting for my two-year-old. As I take a deep breath, I clear away the agenda set for him. I return to the present. I am in the moment with him. It is a meditation for me. I feel in harmony with myself and my son because there's nowhere to go and nothing to do as important as watching the moment unfold together."

"Prayer is imbuing the despised parts of myself with tenderness. I imagine a Renaissance painting, the tender quality of the light, the acceptance of the lines on my face, of my inner darkness and fear. I allow the tender rich antique light to hold and accept the despised parts of myself. Prayer is turning that tender inner light toward others. Seeing clearly who they are, not denying their flaws, yet being kind and courageous enough to speak from the tender illuminated inner space to that which is the same in them."

IMPROVING CONSCIOUS CONTACT

Spirituality is developing conscious contact with our own lives: the decisions we make; the relationships and livelihoods we choose; and the quality of our eating, spending, and being. Spirituality is the process of healing into the moment so that our every thought, word, and action become a prayer and meditation to Life as it flows in and through our lives. Women reflect on how they improve conscious contact with their own lives.

I develop conscious contact with my life by slowing down enough to know what I need. I try not to be a super-achiever. I give myself time to make decisions and permission to make mistakes. I attempt to tune out what society expects of me and I have purged the words "should" and "ought" from my internal voice.

I develop conscious contact with my feelings as I make recovery from food addiction my priority. Abstinence gives me an opportunity to sit with the feelings that come up. I accept them as a part of me. As a result of spending less time obsessing about food, I am faced with my life. I am learning to be present with myself and with others, to know my feelings and to honor theirs.

I develop conscious contact with my life by reflecting on it. I am questioning my source of income. I want my work to support the world as I view it. I wonder about all the time I spend cleaning my house. I think about my love of clothes. It all seems rather wasteful of the world's energy, and my own. But on a smaller scale, I am proud that I have brought much harmony into my life.

I am developing conscious contact with my Inner Wisdom. When I feel the pull of my compulsions around spending, eating, or just wanting a situation to go my way, I get a warning. My heart pounds. I start to feel out of balance. I take a deep breath. It often only takes a second for me to suspend my attachment and open to other possibilities.

COMING INTO ALIGNMENT

As we look back on our lives, we see an unmistakable design flowing from the depths of us in harmony with our gifts, talents, uniqueness, and life purpose. This flow of deep wisdom is faithful even in the midst of difficulties and apparent detours from what is healthy and good. Inner peace comes from trusting the faithfulness of wisdom. We make a daily decision to place ourselves in the middle of this stream of wisdom. Alignment means that we choose to be ourselves this day with no judgment, and live in harmony with the deepest wisdom of our lives. Martha Graham's words inspire us:

> "There is a vitality, a life force, a quickening translated through you into action. And because there is only one of you in all time, this expression is unique. And if you block it, it will never exist through any other medium and it will be lost. The world will not have it. It is not your business to determine how good or valuable it is, nor how it compares to others. It is your business to keep it yours, clearly and directly. To keep the channel open."

Use the following three "Making Conscious Contact" Meditations to improve your conscious contact with Deeper Wisdom and support you to live in alignment with its flow. Simply read them or, if inspired, engage them with breath and movement.

1. Ground of My Being
2. Heart of Life
3. Source of Life

Ground of My Being

A conscious life unfolds from the inside out. Your inner life has been called by many names and known by many images. Breathe into each name and image.

Breathing in... Source of Life,
  Breathing out... My life begins in you.

Breathing in... Ground of My Being,
  Breathing out... My life is rooted in you.

Breathing in... Deeper Wisdom,
  Breathing out... My life unfolds from you.

Breathing in... Truest Self,
  Breathing out... Integrity at the center of my being.

Breathing in... Heart Center,
  Breathing out... Compassion at the center of my being.

Breathing in... Womb Center,
  Breathing out... Creativity at the center of my being.

Breathing in... Inner Sanctuary,
  Breathing out... Stillness at the center of my being.

Breathing in... Sacred Clearing,
  Breathing out... Spaciousness at the center of my being.

Breathing in... Intuition,
  Breathing out... Knowing at the center of my being.

Breathing in... I descend into the deep wisdom of my inner life.
  Breathing out... I assert my will in harmony with its urgings.

As I take a deep breath, I settle into the present moment and reconnect to my inner stillness. In the quietness of here and now, there is peace.

Heart of Life

According to Eastern teachings, the body has seven energy centers called chakras. The fourth chakra is the Heart Center. It is connected to our capacity to love. An acupressure point is located at the Heart Center on the sternum between your breasts. This point supports conscious contact with our emotions. Place your fingertips there.

Begin your day with the "Heart of Life" meditation, which can be as simple as a sitting meditation (as you breathe in harmony with the words of the prayer) or as embodied as a movement meditation (inviting your body to participate in the meditation outlined below). As you become familiar with the words in harmony with your breath, improvise and create your own creative sitting and/or movement meditation.

Breathe in with fingertips on sternum. *Heart of Life,*
> Breathe out as arms open outward. *To you I am opening.*

Breathe in, bringing fingertips to sternum. *Strong is your pulse,*
> Breathe out as arms open outward. *Soothing is your touch.*

Breathe in, bringing fingertips to sternum. *In you,*
> Breathe out as arms open outward. *I feel and flow and live.*

Breathe in with fingertips on sternum. *Heart of Life,*
> Breathe out as arms open outward. *To you I open.*

Breathe in, bringing fingertips to sternum. *Steady is your pulse,*
> Breathe out as arms open outward. *Healing is your touch.*

Breathe in, bringing fingertips to sternum. *In you,*
> Breathe out as arms open outward. *I feel and flow, and live.*

I place myself in the stream of emotion flowing through my life.
I am fully alive.

Source of Life

According to Eastern teachings, the body contains seven energy centers called chakras. The second chakra is located between the pubis and navel and is connected to our creative capacities. An acupressure point is located three finger widths below the belly button. Place your hands on your belly with the tips of your index fingers meeting in the center at the "Sea of Energy" point. This powerful acupressure point strengthens self-confidence. Begin your day with the "Source of Life" meditation.

Sitting with both hands on your belly.

Breathing in: Source of Life,
    Breathing out: To you I come.
Breathing in: Welcoming is your womb,
    Breathing out: Nurturing is your love.
Breathing in: In you,
    Breathing out: I am enclosed and sustained.

Breathe in: Source of Life,
    Breathe out: From you I am pushed.
Breathe in: Strong is your womb.
    Breathe out: Powerful its thrust.
Breathing in: In you,
    Breathing out: I exert, initiate and move.

Through mindful reflection, I place myself in stream of wisdom flowing through my life. I make conscious contact with my truest self and clearest thought.

Chapter 12

In All Your Affairs

Step 12 as Written

Having had a spiritual awakening as a result of these Steps, I carry this message to others and practice these principles in all my affairs.

Step 12 as Rewritten

Having had an awakening as a result of these Steps, I practice ADW's woman-affirming perspectives in all my affairs by living in harmony with my deepest wisdom, truest self, and clearest thought.

Review the information below to be reminded of your journey through the ADW Perspectives and Steps. Use this review as an opportunity to move your experience beyond the page into your life. Staying awake requires ongoing "practice." Mindfulness practice places us in the stream of wisdom flowing through our inner lives, and there, we make conscious contact with our truest self and clearest thought.

Practice the ADW perspectives and steps "in all your affairs" by spending regular time turning inward through mindfulness practice. Practice will assist you to maintain conscious contact with your natural resources: body, breath, and inner life, and to access the resilience embedded within you to apply to every season and situation of your life.

The Perspectives in All Your Affairs

Perspective 1: Your healing task is not to become a new, improved, or changed person. Rather, it is to reclaim your essential self in all its fullness.

Perspective 2: You have discovered the way home to yourself in a quiet descent into the richness of your inner life. In the descent, you have reunited with your essential self and reclaimed your natural resources: body, breath, and inner life.

Perspective 3: You have been empowered by remembering the truth about yourself and by becoming skillful at accessing the resources and resilience embedded within that truth in every season and situation of your life.

Perspective 4: Having discovered the way home, you have embraced the essential connection between self-love and the love of others, and are experiencing your life and relationship from the inside out.

The Steps in All Your Affairs

Step 1: Vulnerability

Step 1: Caught in the swirl of my habits of behavior, I have lost touch with myself and my life has become unmanageable. I reach out for support. This is a brave action on my own behalf.

Step 1 Reminder: Vulnerability and power are not mutually exclusive. Step 1 reminded you of your original power and how to access it to act on your own behalf and gather the resources and support necessary to heal into the present.

Step 1 Affirmation: "I'm vulnerable—some things I cannot change. With vulnerability, I reach out for assistance. This is a brave action on my own behalf. I'm powerful—some things I can change. With courage, I change the things I can."

Step 1 Practice: Use Chapter 3's Mindfulness Meditation "At the Stream of Living Water" in all your affairs. Ours is always a two-fold acknowledgment. Yes, we are limited and finite, and we are powerful and gifted. By applying this two-fold acknowledgement to every situation, challenge, and concern you encounter, you will receive the gift of clarity, which will lead to appropriate strategies and actions.

Step 2: Sanity

Step 2: I have come to believe in the deep wisdom of my own inner life. I stop flailing and am restored to the sanity of a loving and respectful relationship with myself.

Step 2 Reminder: Step 2 reminded you of your inner wisdom and how to access it to define your own spirituality and reclaim your inner sanity and well-being.

Step 2 Affirmation: "I'm learning how to access the deep wisdom of my own inner life. I'm restored to the sanity of a loving and respectful relationship with myself."

Step 2 Practice: Use Chapter 4's "Bring Many Names" in all your affairs. Allow your deep wisdom to awaken appropriate images to provide guidance in every situation, challenge, and concern you encounter. In the process you will receive the gift of sanity, which is accessed in the present moment and released into your experience with each mindful breath, inspiring appropriate strategies and actions.

Step 3: Support

Step 3: I turn my current situation over to the deep wisdom that flows in and through my life. One self-caring step at a time, I unravel my harmful habits of behavior and the thoughts that hold them in place.

Step 3 Reminder: Step 3 reminded you of the support available from within your own inner resources and from the communities of support around you.

Step 3 Affirmation: "I'm learning how to access the resilience of my own inner life. One self-caring step at a time, I unravel my harmful habits of behavior and the thoughts that hold them in place."

Step 3 Practice: Use Chapter 5's Mindfulness Meditation "An Encounter with Deeper Wisdom" in all your affairs. In the encounter, you will receive guidance and support to address every situation, challenge, and concern you encounter. The gift of wisdom is accessed in the present moment and released into your experience with each mindful breath, inspiring appropriate strategies and actions.

Step 4: Self-Awareness

Step 4: Turning a merciful eye toward myself, I inventory both my life-affirming and ineffective habits of behaviors, and identify the habits of thought that inspire them.

Step 4 Reminder: Step 4 reminded you that your interior power is activated by self-awareness and that you grow in self-knowledge by acknowledging the past's influence on the present, walking through the past, and healing into the present.

Step 4 Affirmation: "My interior power is activated by self-awareness. I'm curious and always learning something new about myself."

Step 4 Practice: Use Chapter 7's Inventory Practices in all your affairs. They offer you an opportunity to turn toward your challenges and concerns by surveying your inner territory to understand what's going on. In the process you will "bring harmony back to the conflicting elements" (Thich Nhat Hanh) within you and access your "clearest thought" to identify the resources available to address "all your affairs."

Step 5: Personal Responsibility

Step 5: In the company of trustworthy allies, I celebrate my life-affirming behaviors, accept responsibility for my ineffective behaviors, and make a commitment to my transformation.

Step Reminder: Step 5 reminded you that interior power is strengthened by taking responsibility for your habits of behavior and vowing faithfulness to your own life.

Step 5 Affirmation: "Within a compassionate community, I celebrate my life-affirming behaviors and accept responsibility for my ineffective behaviors. I'm committed to my own transformation."

Step 5 Practice: Step 5 invites us to make a commitment to our own lives and transformation. Writing a "Vow of Faithfulness" is one way to do this. Compose your vow, read it daily, and apply its self-loving perspective to all your affairs. Imagine how a woman who trusts herself and remains loyal to herself, regardless, would address the situations, challenges, or concerns you encounter.

Steps 6 and 7: Readiness and Participation

Step 6 and 7

> I am entirely ready to deepen my inner well-being by relinquishing my negative habits of behavior and cultivating new thoughts to inspire healthier behaviors and outcomes. My life journey is orchestrated by my own inner wisdom. In the fullness of time, I am transformed at a deeper level of my being. I actively participate in this process.

Step 6 and 7 Reminders

> Step 6 reminded you that your life-process is orchestrated by a finely tuned inner timing. When entirely ready, you are freed at a deeper level of your being.

Step 7 reminded you of the importance of staying awake in your own life, meeting each challenge with creativity and taking action on your own behalf with clarity and strength.

Step 6 and 7 Affirmations

"I'm entirely ready to deepen my inner well-being. I cultivate new thoughts to inspire healthier behaviors and outcomes."

"My life journey is orchestrated by my own inner wisdom. I actively participate in my transformation. In the fullness of time, I'm transformed at a deeper level of my being."

Steps 6 and 7 Practice

Use Chapter 8's four-part Mindfulness Practice to identify the formative experiences that shaped the thoughts that hold your ineffective behaviors in place. In the process you will become skillful at cultivating new thoughts that will inspire healthier behaviors and outcomes "in all your affairs."

Step 8 and 9: Relationship Awareness and Responsibility

Steps 8 and 9

Certain that I love myself, I welcome clarity in my relationships. I acknowledge those who were hurt by my ineffective habits of behavior.

Having forgiven myself, I take active responsibility by making amends to those I harmed except when to do so would further injure them or others.

Step 8 and 9 Reminders

Step 8 reminded you of the essential connection between self-love, acceptance, and responsibility and the capacity to create and maintain healthy relationships.

Step 9 reminded you of your own inner courage to repair, reclaim, or bring closure to the relationships that were harmed by your ineffective behaviors.

Step 8 and 9 Affirmations

"Certain that I love myself, I welcome clarity in my relationships."

"Having forgiven myself, I take active responsibility for the consequences of my ineffective behaviors in other people's lives."

Step 8 and 9 Practice

Use Chapter 9's Mindfulness Practices to acknowledge the current and past relationships that are/were harmed by your ineffective behaviors. Access your inner courage to make amends as appropriate. These mindfulness practices will inspire healthier behaviors and outcomes "in all your affairs," and cultivate ongoing accountability to create and maintain healthy relationships.

Step 10: Accountability

Step 10: Choosing to be present in my own life, I acknowledge the gifts and challenges of the day, celebrate my life-affirming behaviors, and take responsibility for my ineffective ones.

Step 10 Reminder: Step 10 reminded you to remain absolutely present in your daily life by turning toward your life each day with mindfulness, accountability, and gratitude.

Step 10 Affirmation: "I'm present in my own life. Today I acknowledge the gifts and challenges of my life with gratitude. I celebrate my life-affirming behaviors. I take responsibility for my ineffective behaviors. I am at peace."

Step 10 Practice: Use Chapter 10's Daily Inventory Practices to reflect upon the blessing and challenge of life and take responsibility for your response to life. The practices enable us to understand the nature of our ineffective behaviors based on resentment and to choose life-affirming behaviors based on gratitude. In the process, your gratitude "muscle" will become stronger, enabling creative strategies, actions, and responses to emerge "in all your affairs."

Step 11: Harmony

Step 11: Through mindful reflection, I place myself in the stream of wisdom flowing through my life. I make conscious contact with my truest self and clearest thought.

Step 11 Reminder: Step 11 reminded you of the necessity of maintaining conscious contact with yourself as you live in harmony from the inside out.

Step 11 Affirmation: "I place myself in the stream of wisdom flowing through my life. I make conscious contact with my truest self and clearest thought. I am at home."

Step 11 Practice: Chapter 11's three "Making Conscious Contact" Meditations place us in the stream of wisdom flowing through our inner lives, and there, we make conscious contact with our truest self and clearest thought. The flow of deep wisdom is faithful even in the midst of difficulties and apparent detours from what is healthy and good. Inner peace "in all your affairs" comes from trusting the faithfulness of your inner wisdom and maintaining your conscious contact with it.

Step 12: Purpose

Step 12: Having had an awakening as a result of these Steps, I practice these principles in all my affairs by living in harmony with my deepest wisdom, truest self, and clearest thought.

Step 12 Reminder: Step 12 reminded you of the purposefulness of a conscious life as it is lived from the inside out in wisdom, truth, and clear thought.

Step 12 Affirmation: "I live in harmony with my deepest wisdom, truest self, and clearest thought. I bring truth, wisdom, and clarity into the world around me. I belong."

Step 12 Practice: Chapter 12 reinforces the necessity of regular mindfulness practice.

Create your own daily mindfulness practice from the many practices introduced in this book. Begin by returning home to your breath, body, and inner life, using this abbreviated version of the "Home is Always Waiting" meditation.

The "Home is Always Waiting" Meditation in All Your Affairs

The "Home is Always Waiting" mindfulness meditation will reach beneath the self-critical noisiness of your mind to the stillness at the center of your being. It invites you to descend into your inner stillness to become re-acquainted with the exquisite resources of your own life: your body, breath, and inner life.

In Chapter 1 you were introduced to the ADW perspective that highlights the meditation. On the next page you will experience the short version of the meditation. You can find a link to the full audio version at www.thegirlgod.com/deeper_wisdom.php. May the HIAW meditation remind you of the truth about yourself when you forget and support you to remain loyal to yourself, no matter what.

Home is always waiting. It is as near as a conscious breath, conscious contact with your woman-body, and a descent into the abundant resources of your inner life. The meaning, recovery, and transformation you seek 'out there' is found within your own heart, mind, body, and life. It is accessed in the present moment and released into your experience with each mindful breath. Return home often—you have everything you need there.

Gather the Gifts of Your Breath

Return home to your breath. Turn your attention inward by taking a few deep breaths. Become conscious of the breath and its faithful rhythm. Savor the breath as it flows in, through, and around you. On each inhalation, gather yourself from the far corners of your life. Bring your energy and attention "home." On each exhalation, release the accumulation of the day. Allow sighs, sounds, and yawns to ride on the back of each exhalation to support you to settle into this moment. Breathing in, *gather*. Breathing out, let go. *Home is always waiting.* Affirm:

> The Breath, from which all life unfolds.
> The Breath, in which past, present, and future meet.
> I receive the gifts of my Breath.

Gather the Gifts of Your Body

Return home to your body. As you continue to breathe deeply, turn your attention toward your body. Make conscious contact with your body: move or stretch it, touch or massage it, or imagine the breath reaching into each part of your body. Meet each body sensation with the breath and your own healing, acknowledging touch. If your attention moves away from home, away from your breath and body, away from this moment, notice the distraction without judgment, and then practice returning home. There will always be distractions. Our life-practice is to return. Breathe again into this moment. Home is always waiting. Affirm:

> The Body, from which all life unfolds.
> The Body, in which past, present, and future meet.
> Body, I gather your gifts.

Gather the Gifts of Your Inner Life

Return home to your inner life. Escorted by the breath and body, we continue our descent. Imagine yourself as a leaf let go of by an autumn tree, a leaf slowly and gradually descending toward the ground, its descent cushioned by the breath of life, a leaf touching the ground in the forest deep within your being. Make conscious contact with the ground of your being through prayer, an expression of openness, a movement, or in the quietness of the breath. Home is always waiting. Affirm:

> The Ground of my Being, from which all life unfolds.
> The Ground, in which past, present, and future meet.
> I receive the gifts of my Inner Life.

A Closing Blessing

Home is always waiting . . .
in tender times and turbulent times, in graceful moments and in awkward situations, in flowing times and in seasons of stagnation, in fullness and in emptiness, in fear and in courage, in trouble and in beauty. Return home often to receive everything that you need to navigate "all your affairs" with clarity, wisdom, and truth.

Gather the gifts of your awakening . . .
Your vulnerability and power; your self-awareness and self-management; your commitment to your own transformation; your presence and participation in your own life; your clarity about your relationships; your deepest wisdom, truest self, and clearest thought . . . and bring them with you into "all your affairs."

Gather the additional resources on the following pages . .
To assist you on your journey: the "Imagine a Woman" poem, mindfulness inspiration, woman-affirming wisdom, and woman-centered recovery groups, always available to you whenever you

need them to heal, grow, and thrive in "all your affairs," one conscious breath at a time.

Finally, with courage and strength, on behalf of the world's children, use the gifts of your awakening to refashion our beloved world by giving birth to images of inclusion, poems of truth, rituals of healing, experiences of transformation, relationships of equality, strategies of peace, institutions of justice, and households of compassion. May it be so.

Imagine a Woman

Until we imagine something, it remains an impossibility. Once imagined, it becomes our experience.

Imagine a woman who loves herself. A woman who gazes with loving kindness upon her past and present, body and needs, ideas and emotions. Whose capacity to love others deepens as she extends loving kindness to herself.

Imagine a woman who accepts herself. A woman who turns a merciful eye toward her own secrets, successes, and shortcomings. Whose capacity to live non-judgmentally deepens as she is merciful toward herself.

Imagine a woman who participates in her own life with interest and attention. A woman who turns inward to listen, remember, and replenish. Whose capacity to be available deepens as she is available to herself.

Imagine a woman who remains faithful to herself through the seasons of life. A woman who preserves allegiance to herself even when opposed. Whose capacity to sustain interest in others deepens as she is loyal to herself.

Imagine a woman who bites into her own life and the fullness of its possibility. A woman who has opened to the depths of goodness within her. Who affirms the original goodness of her children until the stories of old hold no sway in their hearts.

Imagine a community of women who rock the world by giving birth to images of inclusion, poems of truth, rituals of healing, experiences of transformation, relationships of equality, strategies of peace, institutions of justice, and households of compassion for the sake of our children's future.

Imagine a world where the question "what's wrong with me" has been exorcised from the bodies and lives of our daughters. A world where they cultivate their amazing capacities as children of life. Where they travel a less turbulent path than we did toward self-love, self-acceptance, and self-trust.

Imagine yourself as this woman. And together let us imagine such a community and world into being for the sake of our daughters and sons, and our beloved planet.

Inspiration on your Mindfulness Journey...

Mindfulness is... a skill that can be learned.

"Mindfulness is a powerful practice that gives you the tools to build a foundation of clarity and calm in the midst of life's rockiest times. From this place of stability, you can engage the challenges and joys of life with a renewed sense of energy and balance."
-Carol Hendershot

Mindfulness is... accessing the good within you.

"Don't underestimate yourself. You have the ability to wake up. You just need a little bit of practice to be able to touch the understanding and compassion in you. Simple practices such as meditative walking and mindful breathing make this possible."
-Thich Nhat Hanh

Mindfulness is... looking deep within.

"Transformation comes from looking deep within, to a state that exists before fear and isolation arise, the state in which we are inviolably whole just as we are. We connect to ourselves, to our own true experience, and discover there that to be alive means to be whole." -Sharon Salzberg

Mindfulness creates... a refuge of inner stability.

"Through mindfulness practice, we accept with the inevitability of change in our own lives. With acceptance, our fear of change diminishes, and with practice, we achieve true inner stillness, stability, and clarity even in the most turbulent seasons of life." -Patricia Lynn Reilly

Mindfulness is... honoring it all.

"All are welcome. Feelings of compassion and irritation, and acts of planting, eating, and being are honored and offered the same careful attention." -Thich Nhat Hanh

Mindfulness is... de-cluttering the mind.

"Mindfulness helps us get better at seeing the difference between what's happening and the stories we tell ourselves about what's happening. Often such stories treat a fleeting state of mind as if it were our entire and permanent self." -Sharon Salzberg

Mindfulness is... an act of self-love.

"Life is swift and precious while it's in our grasp. Loving yourself is such a small act of appreciation for the everlasting Love that has breathed you into being and on whose wings you will be carried when it's time to leave this life." -Paula M. Reeves

Inspiration on your Woman-Affirming Journey...

"Dear Sisters, please remember: The jewel is in your bosom; Why look for it somewhere else?" -Japanese Folk Zen Saying

"Instead of planting our solitude with our own dream blossoms, we choke the space with continuous music, chatter, and companionship. When the noise stops, there is no inner music to take its place. We must relearn to be alone." -Anne Morrow Lindbergh

"My current view of the world is that life is braided streams of light and darkness, joy and pain, and I just accept them. They both exist and I walk them both. But now I know there is a choice about what I do about them. This awareness is one of the delights of being forty." -Arisika Razak

"When we live from within outward, in touch with our inner power, we become responsible to ourselves in the deepest sense. As we recognize our deepest feelings, we give up being satisfied with suffering and self-negation, and the numbness, which seems like our society's only alternative." -Audre Lorde, *Sister Outsider*

"A woman who echoes Ntosake Shange's dramatic statement, 'I found god in myself and I loved her fiercely,' is saying, 'Female power is strong and creative.' She is saying that the divine principle, the saving and sustaining power, is in herself, that she will no longer look to men or male figures as saviors." -Carol P. Christ

"A true mystic believes that we all have an inward life into which as unto a secret chamber one can retreat at will. In this inner chamber one finds a refuge from the ever-changing aspects of outward existence and from human judgments and distraction. One finds there, repose and a voice which subdues. One finds herself in the presence of her god." -Caroline Stephens

"I will not die an unlived life. I will not live in fear of falling or catching fire. I choose to inhabit my days, to allow my living to open me, to make me less afraid, more accessible, to loosen my heart until it becomes a wing, a torch, a promise. I choose to risk my significance; to live so that which came to me as seed goes to the next as blossom and that which came to me as blossom goes on as fruit." -Dawna Markova

Additional Resources

The **She Recovers** Foundation is a 501(c)(3) non-profit public charity with a growing and evolving community currently consisting of more than 325,000 women in or seeking recovery from substance use disorders, other behavioral health issues and/or life challenges.

This lifeline organization connects women through its virtual platforms and in-person community networks, provides resources and supports women to develop their own holistic recovery patchworks, and empowers them to thrive and share their successes. All efforts are designed to end the stigma and shame often associated with recovery so that more women may heal and grow.

With a special focus on research, the SHE RECOVERS Foundation can also establish a more robust evidence base related to the efficacy of non-traditional recovery pathways.

SHE RECOVERS Foundation stated purpose is to connect, support and empower women in or seeking recovery.

sherecovers.org

Women For Sobriety, Inc. (WFS) is a non-profit organization and a self-help program (also called the New Life Program) for women with Substance Use Disorders. Founded in 1975, it was the first national self-help program for addiction recovery developed to address the unique needs of women. Based upon the thirteen Acceptance Statements, the New Life Program is one of positivity that encourages emotional and spiritual growth. The New Life Program has been extremely effective in helping women to overcome their Substance Use Disorders and learn a whole new lifestyle. As a recovery program, it can stand alone or be used alongside other recovery supports simultaneously.

womenforsobriety.org

Additional Reading

Eating in the Light of the Moon: How Women Can Transform Their Relationship with Food Through Myths, Metaphors, and Storytelling by Anita A. Johnston PhD

In the Realm of Hungry Ghosts: Close Encounters with Addiction by MD Gabor Maté, MD

The Alcohol Experiment: A 30-day, Alcohol-Free Challenge to Interrupt Your Habits and Help You Take Control – Annie Grace

The Courage to Heal: A Guide for Women Survivors of Child Sexual Abuse – Ellen Bass and Laura Davis

This Naked Mind: Control Alcohol, Find Freedom, Discover Happiness & Change Your Life – Annie Grace

Women, Sex and Addiction: A Search for Love and Power by Charlotte Davis Kasl

Please note, this could be a book in and of itself. There are many, many healing books and memoirs available. This list is just a starting point.

If you enjoyed this book, please consider writing a brief review on Amazon and/or Goodreads.

About the Author: Patricia Lynn Reilly, M.Div.

Patricia Lynn Reilly has been inspiring women for over 25 years. Her iconic books, poems, and trainings have traveled around the world. Patricia's earlier books include:

A God Who Looks Like Me: Discovering a Woman-Affirming Spirituality supports you to design a personal spirituality by extending your historical, theological, and personal vision to include the divine feminine. A richly woven tapestry of ritual, story, and history encouraging you to exorcise old images and embrace woman-affirming ones.

Be Full of Yourself: The Journey from Self-Criticism to Self-Celebration dismantles the self-critical question "what's wrong with me" by exploring its historical, theological, and personal origins. Introduces the language of self-celebration.

Imagine a Woman in Love with Herself: Embracing Your Wholeness & Wisdom explores twenty self-affirming qualities, encouraging you to grow in knowledge and love of yourself. Reflections and meditations based on 20 stanzas of the "Imagine a Woman" poem.

I Promise Myself: Making a Commitment to Yourself & Your Dreams refashions the wedding vow and ceremony into a transformational resource for women of all ages. Compose your own vow of faithfulness and create a ceremony of commitment.

Words Made Flesh: An Anthology of Poetry and Prose gives voice to the personal story beneath Patricia's public persona as feminist theologian and inspirational speaker. A celebration of the creativity and resilience of the human spirit.

Love Your Body Regardless: From Body-Judgment to Body-Acceptance – available soon.

www.thegirlgod.com/patricia_lynn_reilly.php

Girl God Books

Original Resistance: Reclaiming Lilith, Reclaiming Ourselves
There is, perhaps, no more powerful archetype of female resistance than Lilith. As women across the globe rise up against the patriarchy, Lilith stands beside them, misogyny's original challenger. This anthology—a chorus of voices hitting chords of defiance, liberation, anger and joy—reclaims the goodness of women bold enough to hold tight to their essence. Through poetry, prose, incantation, prayer and imagery, women from all walks of life invite you to join them in the revolutionary act of claiming their place—of reclaiming themselves.

Re-visioning Medusa: from Monster to Divine Wisdom
A remarkable collection of essays, poems, and art by scholars who have researched Her, artists who have envisioned Her, and women who have known Her in their personal story. All have spoken with Her and share something of their communion in this anthology.

New Love: a reprogramming toolbox for undoing the knots
A powerful combination of emotional/spiritual techniques, art and inspiring words for women who wish to move away from patriarchal thought. *New Love* includes a mixture of compelling thoughts and suggestions for each day, along with a "toolbox" to help you change the parts of your life you want to heal.

The Girl God
A book for children young and old, celebrating the Divine Female by Trista Hendren. Magically illustrated by Elisabeth Slettnes with quotes from various faith traditions and feminist thinkers.

See a complete list at **www.thegirlgod.com**